Learning English/ Learning America

Voices of Latinos and Asian Americans

Juana Mora
Gina Masequesmay
Eunai Shrake
Ana Sánchez Muñoz

CALIFORNIA STATE UNIVERSITY, NORTHRIDGE

KENDALL/HUNT PUBLISHING COMPANY
4050 Westmark Drive   Dubuque, Iowa 52002

CONTENTS

FOREWORD

KRIS D. GUTIÉRREZ

The issue of immigration is one of those hot-button issues that evokes a range of sentiments, especially in states and communities experiencing significant demographic shifts. In times of heightened economic hardship and limited opportunity, the rhetoric of xenophobia and anti-immigrant sentiment in communities marked by demographic change is intensified. Immigrants—and their practices—are often caricaturized as aliens who drain the economy, provide little value-added, and who share few common practices and values with dominant communities. Such unexamined and flat narratives about groups of people are troubling on many levels. First, sweeping generalizations about communities and their members are not very useful as they fail to capture the nuances of people's everyday lives, their range of experiences, or the available resources and constraints of their ecologies. Second, the racialized character of segments of the public discourse help to sustain deficit portraits of immigrants while minimizing the significant diversity within cultural communities and the notable points of regularity across communities. And this, of course, is the point and contribution of this volume, *Learning English/Learning America: Voices of Latinos and Asian Americans.*

Of relevance to the topic of this book, the emergence of new or expanded cultural and linguistic communities has posed new challenges for an educational system that is largely unprepared to address the needs of diasporic communities who bring new experiences, practices, and histories to their schooling experiences. Further, helping immigrant students develop rich toolkits that expand what they know is constrained by educational reform policies that emphasize narrow notions of language and literacy learning. Language and literacy programs that define the curriculum for many children of languages other than English are organized as one-size-fits all programs; specifically, the "sameness as fairness" principle undergirding much of current educational reform promotes a normative view of children living in poverty, their learning needs, their communities' language practices, and identities as weak and incompetent students.[1] As I have written elsewhere, contemporary theorizations of nondominant communities often work together with reductive and static notions of culture and poverty to construct deficit explanations of the "underachievement" of nondominant students, especially in core subject areas like literacy and language learning.[2]

---

[1] K. Gutiérrez and N. Jaramillo, "Looking for Educational Equity: The Consequences of Relying on *Brown*." In *With More Deliberate Speed: Achieving Equity and Excellence in Education-Realizing the Full Potential of Brown v. Board of Education*, ed. A. Ball, 173-189 (Malden, MA: Blackwell, 2006).

[2] K. Gutiérrez and B. Rogoff, "Cultural Ways of Learning: Individual Traits or Repertoires of Practice." *Educational Researcher*, 32 (5) (2003): 19–25.

As the narratives in *Learning English/Learning America* so richly portray, immigrants must navigate new practices and the challenges that come with intercultural exchange and interaction. Authors Mora, Masequesmay, Shrake, and Sánchez Muñoz advance productive strategies and views for more expansive language-learning approaches by grounding their work in narratives of diverse Asian and Latina/o community members who experienced the processes of immigration and transmigration and negotiated a range of developmental tasks—tasks that are generally not factored into theories of learning and development or classroom pedagogies. From "Coming to America: The Immigrant Journey," to "Learning English," and "Acculturation and Changing Identity," we are introduced to individual stories of hardship, alienation, and resilience from which we can begin to understand better the regularity of experiences shared by members of Latino/a and Asian cultural communities. But equally as important, these stories also make visible the significant variance in how individuals develop adaptive strategies to assist their movement across borders—national, linguistic, and cultural.

Language plays a powerful role in the border crossing that immigrant life entails. This book brings together a collection of perspectives on language learning that makes immigrants' narratives the standpoint from which to begin to understand and develop new pedagogies of hope and possibility for new student populations. Understanding the complexity of transcultural life in a cultural and political context that defines diversity and difference as problems to be eliminated or fixed will help educators develop fuller portraits of immigrant communities, their experiences, and the toolkits they draw on to navigate everyday life. I believe this collection can serve as a catalyst for new conversation and transformation of extant, unproductive views of student learners to more robust views of students from nondominant communities who have a range of experiences, including the learning that comes with immigration and the various boundary crossings it entails. Understanding how students develop what Barbara Rogoff and I call "repertoires of practice" will make it easier to push back against simplistic and essentialist views of students and to develop respectful pedagogies that assist students to reach their full potential, academically and beyond.

ACKNOWLEDGMENTS

This book project originated with Dr. Sandra Chong, our colleague at California State University, Northridge. Having been touched by many of her students' stories of struggles journeying to America and adapting to a new culture and language, she thought of collecting these stories to share with other students and teachers. Dr. Juana Mora and Dr. Gina Masequesmay were recruited to the project. As the project evolved, we now have Dr. Ana Sánchez Muñoz and Dr. Eunai Shrake as co-editors along with Dr. Mora and Dr. Masequesmay. Dr. Chong, unfortunately due to other commitments, did not participate in this first collection. We hope, however, that she will be able to participate in future planned collections with different focuses and emphases. We want to thank all the contributors for sharing their stories. We also want to thank Joseph Wells, our acquisition editor, and Ryan L. Schrodt, our project coordinator, for their support and encouragement. We also want to thank and acknowledge the art work of Yreina Cervantez, who designed our book cover. Most of all, we want to thank Dr. Chong for her original idea and initiative on this project.

INTRODUCTION

Learning from Our Struggles

GINA MASEQUESMAY AND JUANA MORA

We, the editors of this book, are faculty at California State University, Northridge. We teach undergraduate courses on Asian American and Latino immigrant children and education. Some of us have been teaching these courses for nearly 20 years and others are just beginning this teaching journey. English is the second language for all of us and we are also immigrants to this nation. Because of our own immigrant experiences, we believe in the importance of understanding the lived experiences, cultural values, and strengths of immigrants and their families. Given this shared belief, we compiled this collection of Latino and Asian American immigrant stories about coming to the United States, learning a new language, and forming a new identity. We compiled these testimonies of change and struggle because we hear these stories in our classrooms and in our offices and read about them in our students' papers. We have students in our courses who come from China, Vietnam, Korea, Cambodia, Central America, and Mexico. There are also students who are not immigrants themselves, but are second- or third-generation children of immigrants. Yet they share similar tales of struggle in navigating between the dominant culture and their often marginalized ethnic cultures.

These immigrant students and children of non-English-speaking parents sometimes struggle in our classes, working twice as hard as native English-speaking students to achieve and excel. They are conscientious students who work to help their families and study to fulfill the "American dream." They come to the United States to seek better economic and educational opportunities, others leave their hometowns to flee a dangerous political situation, and some come to join family members. In class, they are at times still fearful or shy about speaking English. Their "stories" and "family stories" about coming to America, learning English, and adapting to American life are important considering the large numbers of younger immigrants in California's elementary and middle schools. In California today, *59.4 percent*[1] of the total school-age population is either Asian or Latino. The stories in our collection highlight some of the struggles that more than half of California's primary to secondary school students may be experiencing. We believe that these stories can help teachers and other adults understand the emotional, cultural, and linguistic barriers that our students face on a daily basis. These stories may help teachers and other service professionals learn how to be more supportive of students who are immigrants or children of immigrants and their struggles to learn a new language, adapt to a new culture, and make sense of what to do about their

---

[1] www.ed-data.k12.ca.us.

native culture. Furthermore, we hope our stories will help other Asian and Latino Americans empower themselves to deal with their current challenges.

We begin our documentation of the Latino and Asian immigrant experiences with the stories about the journey itself—about the various ways that Latinos and Asians come to the United States. All speak about the difficulties of the specific journey, how they actually got here, whether they cross a desert on foot or escape their country on a boat. For Latinos, sometimes the journey is as safe and simple as a flight from a city in Mexico to a city in the United States, and sometimes it is a dangerous crossing of the border by walking miles across a desert. For Asians, depending on the economic and political conditions of the country of origin at the time of immigration, the journey may be on a makeshift boat or a plane or by walking through the jungle. Then, there are the stories about how much they miss family, friends, and familiar surroundings they left behind. The sadness in these stories over family and friends who are now no longer a part of their daily lives is sometimes beyond understanding. The loss is overwhelming, particularly in light of living in a new country sometimes with strangers, sometimes with distant family, often with multiple families living under one roof. The journeys sometimes take place over generations, beginning with the journey of the grandparents, then the parents, then children. There are also stories of new forms of immigration that are more "cyclical" and short term in nature whereby families come to the United States temporarily to make some money, then return to the country of origin.

We next document the experiences of linguistic adaptation of Latino and Asian immigrants and their children as they slowly learn English. We were interested in illustrating the process of learning new sounds, new vocabularies, and new ways of communication. We wanted to know how it feels to be silenced by not knowing what others are saying to you, what impeded or facilitated the acquisition of English, and how it feels to be born in the United States but to be placed in ESL classes. There are stories about how not knowing the language silences the newcomer out of fear, out of not knowing how to make new sounds and words, and the embarrassment of saying things incorrectly and being laughed at by people around you. For those of us who work with immigrant students and families, it is important to understand that one of the most difficult aspects of learning English in America is that it threatens to completely erase the native language and culture. In the U.S. educational system, there is a history of the promotion of complete "assimilation" by learning English often at the expense of the native language and culture. Many immigrant children, while not able to verbalize this, feel this tension between their two languages and cultures and need help in understanding this process. We hope that these stories will highlight the difficult transitions that immigrant children make as they navigate a new language and new surroundings.

Finally, we address another aspect of immigrating to America that involves social, economic, cultural, and political adaptation and the formation of new identities. It refers to the process of learning American ways of life and also figuring out what it means to become an ethnic "American" in America. The stories tell about struggling with questions such as, am I Mexican or American? Chinese or American? The stories tell about struggles to answer these questions and to integrate two ways of thinking, being, and behaving and two sets of cultural expectations. As you will read in this section called, "Who Am I: Acculturation and Identity Change," this is a long-term process that is constantly changing with new demographic trends, massive immigration to different parts of the world, and global forms of cultural contact.

To many, America is the land of opportunity and education is the stepping stone to success in America. As teachers or future teachers, we are de facto gatekeepers to many people in realizing their American dreams. With this important responsibility, a better understanding of who are some of our immigrants today is crucial in facilitating their successes. This book is a compilation of stories by Asian Americans and Latinos about their experiences in the school system. We organized the stories into tales of immigration in a section called *Coming to America: The Immigrant Journey;* accounts of language acquisition in a section called *Learning English;* and stories about acculturation and identity in the last section, *Who Am I: Acculturation and Identity Change.* We hope through the sharing of these experiences, teachers and future teachers can have better insights about their immigrant students' struggles and in that revelation be able to facilitate their students in overcoming obstacles that impede them from realizing their potential and in achieving their "American dream."

This introductory chapter will share with the readers some demographic trends, particularly in California. We believe this background information is important in providing a broader context to understand the population of students we are teaching. After the introduction chapter, we present the stories in thematic order of migration, language acquisition, and acculturation. For each of the sections, there is an overview of relevant background information to frame and highlight some of the main issues about each particular section's topic. In each of the stories, we asked the authors not only to share their struggles but also to tell who or what helped them in overcoming hurdles, and their recommendations to future teachers. With this in mind, we hope these true and personal stories will be compelling to readers to begin a process of reexamining how he or she can create a classroom that is more open and supportive of its more vulnerable students. Finally, we summarize common themes across these stories and make our concluding remarks. In the last section, we provide a list of recommended readings.

Demographic Trends

According to the U.S. Census Bureau's *Population Trends in the 20th Century,* in 1900, one in eight Americans was of a race other than white[2]. In 2000, one in four is nonwhite. Where the population of the nation has more than tripled, the biggest shift in

---

[2] Frank Hobbs and Nicole Stoops, *Demographic Trends in the 20th Century,* U.S. Census Bureau, Census 2000 Special Reports, Series CENSR-4 (Washington, DC: U.S. Government Printing Office, 2002).

racial diversity occurred in the latter half of the twentieth century, highlighted by the liberalization of immigration laws particularly with the Immigration and Naturalization Act of 1965 that allowed for the significant increase in Asian and Latino immigrants to the United States.[3] Unlike the past, when immigration for these two groups was more for labor purposes that recruited mostly young men for hard, manual labor, the new legislation allowed for family reunification. This permitted more women to immigrate to the United States and let families and communities grow. In sync with the changing labor market that needed not just cheap labor for manual work, the new economy also demanded workers with high education and skills to fill the professional jobs along with low-skilled workers for the expanding service sector. With continuous and growing U.S. intervention in world politics, we not only have immigrants coming here for jobs and family reunification but also for political asylum. Whereas Asian immigrants are represented by both high-skilled and low-skilled workers and refugees, Latino immigrants, particularly from Mexico, are represented primarily by low-skilled workers, and Central Americans are overrepresented by political refugees.

Beginning in the 1960s, we have seen a historic population growth in numbers and percentages of Asian and Latino immigrants in the western United States that has reshaped our nation's cities, towns, and schools. In addition to changing immigration laws that are more open and less restrictive, U.S. involvement in Southeast Asia and its aftermath in the 1970s and U.S. involvement in Central America and its economic and political impact in the 1980s have contributed to a dramatic growth of these two populations in the United States. As presented in Figure 1, from 1980 to 2000, for example, the Latino population more than doubled in the United States making Latinos commensurate to African Americans in U.S. population percentage, growing from 6.4% to 12.5% or from 14.6 million to 35.3 million people.[4] The Asian American population also increased during this time.[5] Despite making up a smaller percentage of the U.S. population (at least 3.6% or 10.2 million, which does not include "Hapas" or mixed race Asian Americans), Asian Americans had the greatest percentage change in population growth of all races. This has resulted in the establishment of landmarks such as Little Saigon, Little Phnom Penh, Koreatown, and Little India to American cities that until the 1980s, knew only Chinatowns, Little Tokyos, and Filipino Towns. With 204% change, the Asian American population has basically tripled within two decades.

---

[3] Paul Ong and John M. Liu. "U.S. Immigration Policies and Asian Migration." In *Contemporary Asian America: A Multidisciplinary Reader*, ed. M. Zhou and J. V. Gatewood, 155-174 (New York: New York University Press, 2000).

[4] Ibid., 78.

[5] Ibid., 79.

Figure 1: Percent Change in Population Size by Race and Hispanic Origin: 1980 to 2000

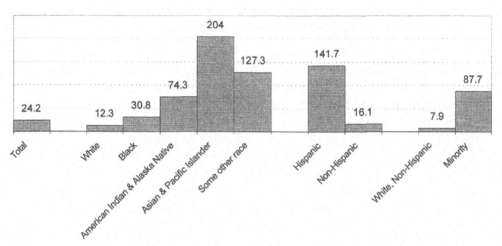

Source: US Census Bureau, Decennial Census of Population, 1980 to 2000.

More interestingly, most of these trends have taken place primarily in California, which has a larger number of Asian and Latino residents than any other state in the nation. We estimated from the 2000 Census that 30.1% of all Latinos and 36.1% of all Asian Americans in the United States live in California. Considering that California in 2004 had the highest number of elementary school-age children (4.8 million), the highest number of high school-age children (2.1 million), the highest number of adult residents (26.3 million), and the highest number of people 65 and older (3.8 million),[6] public servants and other professionals must address the issues of diversity in languages and cultures to better understand their new constituents. The drastic change in demographics is especially felt in Los Angeles County and the city of Los Angeles. The Los Angeles-Long Beach-Santa Ana metro area is sixth in the nation in highest numerical growth with a 771,314 increase and is the second only to the New York metro area as most populous metro area in the country, with 13 million people.[7] Based on census data, we estimated that 12% of all Latinos and 11% of all Asian Americans in the nation reside in Los

---

[6] Census Bureau Estimates of Number of Children and Adults in the States and Puerto Rico. Downloaded on 12/16/07 from URL: http://www.census.gov/Press-Release/www/releases/archives/population/004083.html.

[7] U.S. Census Bureau News, 50 Fastest-Growing Metro Areas Concentrated in West and South. Released on April 1, 2000-July 1, 2006. Downloaded on 12/16/07 from URL: http://www.census.gov/Press-Release/www/releases/archives/population/009865.html.

Angeles County (LACO). More interestingly, Latinos make up 32.4% of California's population while Asians make up 10.9%. This trend continues at the Los Angeles county level with Latinos at 44.6% and Asians at 12%. At the city level, the percentage of Asians decreases to 10% but the Latinos increase to 46.5%.

In California, 26% of the population is foreign born. Within the Asian American community, 66% are foreign born at the state level, 69% at the county level, and 71% at the city level. For Latinos, the numbers are 43%, 49%, and 56% from state, to county to municipality. Not surprisingly, 37% of the California population, 50% of Los Angeles County, and 53% of the city of Los Angeles speak a language other than English at home. For the Latino and Asian American population, the percentage of people speaking a language other than English is 70% to 79%. Given these trends, it is crucial for those of us who are teachers or planning to be teachers to understand the new and much more diverse population of students who are coming to our classrooms if we are to effectively address their language, education, and cultural needs.

English Language Learners in California Schools

These demographic changes in California are reflected in the number of children in California schools who are immigrant, foreign born, and classified as English language learners. The table below indicates that the Latino and Asian/Pacific Islander student population combined represents 59% of the total K–12 student population in California.

K-12 Student Enrollment by Ethnicity
State of California, 2006-2007[8]

	Enrollment	Percent Total
Native American	48,383	0.8%
Asian/Pacific Islander	714,712	11.3%
Latino	3,026,956	48.1%
African American	477,776	7.6%
White	1,849,078	29.4%
Multiple/No Response	170,038	2.7%
Total	6,286,943	100%

---

[8] www.ed-data.k12.ca.us.

According to the following table, at least 25% of these students speak a language other than English.

Languages of English Learners in California Schools
State of California, 2006–2007

	Number of Students	Percent of Enrollment
Spanish	1,338,611	21.3%
Vietnamese	34,356	0.5%
Filipino (Pilipino or Tagalog)	21,435	0.3%
Cantonese	21,388	0.3%
Hmong	21,047	0.3%
Other	131,824	2.1%
Total	1,568,661	25.0%

Why Latino and Asian Stories?

We explored Asian and Latino immigrant experiences for several reasons. First, our students in our classrooms are primarily Asian and Latino, reflecting California's demographics. Also, two of us teach in the Asian American Studies Department and two of us teach in the Chicana/o Studies Department; thus, our expertise blends well with our teaching and with our students. More important, we wanted to emphasize both the similarities and the uniqueness of Latino and Asian American immigrant experiences, and how these experiences may impact immigrants' educational trajectories. Latinos and Asians share the difficult journeys of coming to America. Their stories, their fears, and the reasons for making the difficult journey are similar. All want a better life and better educational opportunities for their children, and some Asians—like Central Americans—flee an unsafe political or military environment. As these two groups arrive and slowly begin to make a life in America, they share similar struggles with learning a new language and adjusting to a new cultural environment. Many share the embarrassment of saying the wrong thing or making English sounds with an "accent." Almost all speak about going through a stage of being silent, feeling mute and isolated. There are also many similarities between Asians and Latinos regarding the process of acculturation and deciphering what parts of their culture to keep and what parts of the new culture to adapt and when and how to "perform" these multiple cultural behaviors and identities. Overall, we have learned through our students that Latinos and Asians have similar experiences in U.S. classrooms, experiencing the same sense of lack of understanding and neglect from the majority educational system.

We find in these stories that Asian and Latino immigrants undergo great struggles to adapt to a new culture, learn English, and find ways to honor their cultural roots and traditions at the same time they become members of this society. We are learning from these stories that old theoretical models of identity and acculturation may not capture what is taking place today. We find that there are Asians and Latinos who have found ways to become "transnational" citizens of two countries and cultures. Some maintain their ties to their home country or hometown, often sending money back home but also visiting regularly, sometimes returning to the hometown for important life cycle rituals and events and then celebrating these in the United States as well. Learning a new language may also be different in a new global age where communication and access to information is much more advanced than in the past. More recent immigrants come to this country perhaps now with some exposure to English and "the American culture," even if it is culture as expressed through mass media. All of this is new and Asians and Latinos are at the forefront of making new changes in their own lives and in our nation's cultural identity.

Section 1

COMING TO AMERICA
The Immigrant Journey

Introduction to the Section by Eunai Shrake

This theoretical piece introduces key concepts in international migration, a brief history of Asian and Latino immigration, and struggles and challenges these immigrants face before, during, and after migration that provide contexts for the students' immigration stories presented in this section.

Push/Pull Factors in International Migration

Immigration to America has been the dream of many people for the past couple of centuries. While the early immigrants to the United States were overwhelmingly of European origin (with the exception of African Americans who were forced into migration as slaves), the vast majority of contemporary immigrants have their origins in either Asia or Latin America. Although the scope and character of immigration to the United States have undergone some changes, the reasons for immigration have not changed much.

The classic model of international migration explains that typically international migration is caused by a combination of "push" and "pull" factors. Push factors refer to the immigrants' motives or conditions for leaving their country of origin, while pull factors refer to alluring characteristics of the receiving country that attract people in. Traditionally, dire economic conditions, political instability, and religious persecution in the sending countries have been the major factors that push people out of their countries. Corresponding to these push factors, the prospect of greater economic opportunities, greater political as well as religious freedom, and better overall opportunities in the receiving countries have been relevant pull factors.

Since the majority of the immigration to America is economic migration, a quest for greater economic opportunities has been a primary motivation of people who come to America. For example, the acute push factors that result in immigration from Mexico are mostly related to economic conditions in Mexico such as overpopulation, un- or under-employment, and recurring economic crises.[1] In the case of economic migration, immigrants come to America because they believe that their move would result in a considerable economic improvement. In other words, the seeming possibility of realizing the so-called American dream (the availability of jobs and higher living standards) has been the primary pull factor while the economic crisis has been the push factor.

In addition to the economic motivation, a search for a better educational opportunity for children is another powerful motivation for migration to America. In fact, many

---

[1] David Maciel and Maria Herrera-Sobek, "Introduction: Cultures across Borders," in *Culture across Borders: Mexican Immigration and Popular Culture*, ed. David Maciel and Maria Herrera-Sobek, 3—24 (Tucson: University of Arizona Press, 1998).

recent Latino and Asian immigrants often state that the most important reason for their decision to immigrate to America is to provide a better education for their children. This motivation is particularly strong for recent immigrants from East Asian countries such as Taiwan, Korea, and Japan; it is attributed to the extremely competitive educational systems in these countries that put young children under immense pressure to excel in many standardized tests and entrance examinations if they are to enter prestigious universities. To prepare for those tests and examinations, it is not unusual for many young people to go through extensive cram schools and private tutoring in addition to already long hours of regular schools. This condition is often called "examination hell" and the whole process of competition is considered a rite of passage for young ones to get into adulthood. This situation prompts many middle-class Asian families to abandon their homeland primarily in search of better education for their children.

Another noneconomic push factor includes political or religious persecution, which often results in ethnic cleansing, genocide, and civil war. For instance, Cuban refugees between 1965 and 1973; large numbers of Southeast Asian refugees from Vietnam, Laos, and Cambodia following the fall of South Vietnam since 1975; and Central American refugees throughout the 1980s and 1990s were pushed by political motives to escape persecution from communist regimes.

The push-pull model seems wonderfully simple; nevertheless, it masks the tremendous complexity of forces that create the push-pull dynamics.[2] Asian and Latino immigrants, on the whole, share various push-pull factors for migration. However, there is still extraordinary diversity in motives, modes of passage to America, and the contexts of exit and reception. This diversity is caused by differing immigrants' socioeconomic status; as professionals, entrepreneurs, and manual laborers, and their legal-political status when they enter; as documented, undocumented, and refugees.[3] In this section, students' stories of the journey clearly demonstrate this diversity as to why and how they came to America. James Van's and Thuy Le's stories represent the Southeast Asian refugee experience; Hye-Young Kwon's and Lingga Oka's stories depict the post-1965 Asian immigration experience. Yesenia Sanchez and Victor Zuniga tell of immigration from Latin America as documented and undocumented newcomers, respectively, while Lucia Castillo documents three generations' journey to the United States as both illegal and legal immigrants.

---

[2] David Engstrom, "Hispanic Immigration at the New Millennium," in *Chicana/o Studies: Survey and Analysis*, ed. Dennis Bixler-Marquez, Carlos Ortega, and Rosalia Torres, 223–240 (Dubuque, IA: Kendall/Hunt, 2007).

[3] Ruben Rumbaut, "Origins and Destinies: Immigration to the United States since World War II," in *New American Destinies: A Reader in Contemporary Asian and Latino*, ed. Darrell Hamamoto and Rodolfo Torres, 15–46 (New York: Routledge, 1997).

A Brief History of Asian and Latino Immigration

The history of Asian immigration to America can be divided generally into two periods: pre-1965 and post-1965 immigration. The pre-1965 immigration began with the first large-scale Chinese immigration during 1849–1882. Early Chinese immigrants worked in the various minefields in California and later on the transcontinental railroad. Early Chinese immigrants also worked on Louisiana's sugar plantations after the Civil War. When the Chinese were banned from entering America with the passage of the Chinese Exclusion Act of 1882, they were replaced by the Japanese, Koreans, Asian Indians, and Filipinos in the late 19th and the early twentieth century. Most of them were recruited to fill the labor needs in sugar plantations in Hawai'i and agricultural fields in California. These early Asians in America were largely bachelor communities of sojourners with the exception of the Japanese who were allowed to bring their families. Asian American children, other than the *Nisei,* or second-generation Japanese Americans, in those early years were rare. With the passage of anti-Asian immigration legislation such as the Gentleman's Agreement in 1907 and the Asiatic Barred Zone Act of 1917, Asian immigration to America virtually ended for the next 50 years.

The watershed for Asian immigration came with the passage of the new Immigration Act in 1965, which ended racial restrictions on migration. This act, in combination with the Indochinese Refugee Act in 1975, resulted in a rapid influx of immigrants from Asia, leading to an explosive population growth accompanied by tremendous diversity in ethnicity and nativity in the Asian American community. The 1970 census counted only 1.5 million Asian Americans, compared with 13.2 million in 2005.[4] This amounts to a ninefold increase in little more than 30 years. Through 1960, the Chinese and Japanese represented the majority of the Asian American population. Currently, the five largest Asian American groups are Chinese, Filipino, Asian Indian, Vietnamese, and Korean. Studies show that post-1965 Asian immigrants tend to be middle class, educated, and urban compared to their pre-1965 counterparts[5] with the exception of half the refugee population from Laos, Cambodia, and Vietnam. At this point in U.S. history, the majority of the Asian American population is foreign-born and they are the most diverse ethnic group in the United States in terms of language, ethnicity, and religion.

Latino immigration has a long history dating back to the late nineteenth century when thousands of Mexican workers immigrated to Texas, California, New Mexico, and other American states that had belonged to Mexico until the war that resulted in conquest. However, the large-scale Latino immigration occurred with the implementation of the Bracero Program that allowed tens of thousands of Mexican

---

[4] http://www.infoplease.com/ipa/A0762156.html.

[5] Timothy Fong, "The History of Asians in America," in *Asian Americans: Experiences and Perspectives,* ed. Timothy Fong and Larry Shinagawa, 13–30 (Upper Saddle River, NJ: Prentice Hall, 2000).

agricultural workers to work temporarily in the United States between 1942 and 1964. After the program was terminated, some braceros overstayed their work visas and their wives and children followed them north.[6] The Bracero Program helped establish employment and social networks in the Mexican American community that facilitated a continuous flow of Latino immigration well after the program ended in 1964.[7]

In the 1970s and 1980s, the Latino American community experienced dramatic population growth and great internal diversity as well. In other words, the Latino American population has become more numerous and more diverse in its ethnic composition since the 1970s.[8] Similar to Asian immigration, the large influx of Latino American immigration was greatly influenced by the Immigration Act of 1965 and the Refugee Act in 1980. The family reunification provisions in the 1965 Immigration Act resulted in a chain migration that has accounted for a preponderance of all non-refugee migration from Latin America, and the Refugee Act has provided the dominant route for high refugee flows from Central American countries.

Along with high levels of legal immigration, undocumented immigration also emerged as the chief alternative immigration route in the late 1970s and 1980s. Due to Mexico's failing economy coupled with continued political conflict in Central America, the pressure to emigrate in this region had intensified. Even when the means by which they could legally enter the United States was exhausted, immigrants continued to come, with or without visas, thus creating a growing illegal immigration flow.[9] Upon arrival, disproportionate numbers of these undocumented immigrants work as low-wage laborers, occupying the bottom tier of the United States' manufacturing and service sectors.

By the 1980s more than four-fifths of all legal immigrants came from either Asia or Latin America. If we could somehow include illegal immigrants in the calculations, this figure would undoubtedly exceed nine-tenths.[10] Such a pattern is likely to continue as long as U.S. immigration law remains essentially as it is and economic and social conditions in most of Asia and Latin America don't change much.

---

[6] Pierrette Hongagneu-Sotelo, "Families on the Frontier: From Braceros in the Fields to Braceras in the Home," in *Chicanas/Chicanos at the Crossroads: Social, Economic and Political Change*, ed. David Maciel and Isidro Ortiz, 259–273 (Tucson: University of Arizona Press, 1996).

[7] Engstrom, "Hispanic Immigration."

[8] Leo Chavez and Rebecca Martinez, "Mexican Immigration in the 1980s and Beyond," in *Chicanas/Chicanos at the Crossroad: Social, Economic and Political Change*, ed. David Maciel and Isidro Ortiz, 25–51 (Tucson: University of Arizona Press, 1996).

[9] Engstrom, "Hispanic Immigration."

[10] Roger Daniels, "United States Policy Towards Asian Immigration: Contemporary Developments in Historical Perspective," in *New American Destinies: A Reader in Contemporary Asian and Latino*, ed. Darrell Hamamoto and Rodolfo Torres, 73–89 (New York: Routledge, 1994).

Struggles and Challenges

Regardless of why, when, and how they come to America, most Asian and Latino immigrants experience certain challenges and obstacles before, during, and after their journey. Premigration difficulties include the emigration policies of some sending countries that may make acquiring exit visas difficult (e.g., Cuba) and psychological difficulties associated with separating from family members and friends and leaving familiar social networks behind. During the journey, many immigrants struggle with emotional anxiety over an uncertain future in America and other traumatic experiences often experienced by refugees and some border crossers. As Thuy Le and James Van describe their parents' journey as "boat people" and "land people," respectively, many Southeast Asian refugees suffered greatly from starvation, bad weather, and attacks by pirates. Similarly, illegal immigrants from the U.S.-Mexican border often suffer from the harrowing experience of crossing the desert and from the fear of being caught by the border patrol. Postmigration challenges include dealing with negative perceptions of both legal and illegal immigration by the general public in the mainstream society (e.g., California's Proposition 187[11]), culture shock, acquiring a new language, and acculturation pressure and its resultant generational conflict between first-generation parents and second-generation children. Students' stories of journey in this section also mention, albeit briefly, these issues of acculturation/adaptation difficulties.

Considering that an increasingly high proportion of recent immigrants are coming from Asia and Latin America, the well-being of Asian American and Latino immigrants and their children in America will greatly influence the general health and welfare of the American society. Educating and assisting these immigrants to become incorporated into the fabric of American life would be a smart investment in America's future.[12]

The essays in this section offer important insights into the diverse backgrounds of Latino and Asian American immigrants and their children and the need to recognize and appreciate the struggles and challenges they have faced. It is our hope that the review of these stories of Latino and Asian American experiences will help future teachers sensitize themselves to the students' immigrant backgrounds and appreciate the multicultural dynamics in the classroom of the twenty-first century.

---

[11] California Proposition 187 was a 1994 ballot initiative designed to deny some health and social services, including access to public education to illegal aliens in California. It passed with over 58 percent of the vote, but was overturned by a federal court.

[12] Engstrom, "Hispanic Immigration."

Bibliography

Chavez, Leo and Rebecca G. Martinez. "Mexican Immigration in the 1980s and Beyond." In *Chicanas/Chicanos at the Crossroads: Social, Economic and Political Change,* edited by David Maciel and Isidro Ortiz, 25–51. Tucson: University of Arizona Press, 1996.

Daniels, Roger. "United States Policy Towards Asian Immigration: Contemporary Developments in Historical Perspective." In *New American Destinies: A Reader in Contemporary Asian and Latino,* edited by Darrell Hamamoto and Rodolfo Torres, 73–89. New York: Routledge, 1994.

Engstrom, David. "Hispanic Immigration at the New Millennium." In *Chicana/o Studies: Survey and Analysis,* edited by Dennis Bixler-Marquez, Carlos Ortega, and Rosalia Torres, 223–240. Dubuque, IA: Kendall/Hunt, 2007.

Fong, Timothy. "The History of Asians in America." In *Asian Americans: Experiences and Perspectives,* edited by Timothy Fong and Larry Shinagawa, 13–30. Upper Saddle River, NJ: Prentice Hall, 2000.

Hondagneu-Sotelo, Pierrette. "Families on the Frontier: From Braceros in the Fields to Braceras in the Home." In *Chicanas/Chicanos at the Crossroads: Social, Economic and Political Change,* edited by David Maciel and Isidro Ortiz, 259–273. Tucson: University of Arizona Press, 1996.

Maciel, David and Maria Herrera-Sobek. "Introduction: Cultures across Borders." In *Culture across Borders: Mexican Immigration and Popular Culture*, edited by David Maciel and Maria Herrera-Sobek, 3–24. Tucson: University of Arizona Press, 1998.

Rumbaut, Ruben. "Origins and Destinies: Immigration to the United States since World War II" In *New American Destinies: A Reader in Contemporary Asian and Latino,* edited by Darrell Hamamoto and Rodolfo Torres, 15–46. New York: Routledge, 1997.

A Lottery to Opportunity

—LINGGA OKA

One day in October 1989, I read in a newspaper about U.S. green card lotteries being offered. The application had to be sent to the United States within the week of November 11 to November 19, 1989. The program was called NP-5 and it still exists under a different name: Diversity Visa Program.[13]

My husband and I applied right away and sent three application letters, one letter each day, hoping that one of them would arrive between November 11 and November 19, 1989. Six months later, we got a letter telling us that we had won the green card lottery and that to continue with the application process, we had to provide certified translations of all documents and have an interview with the American Embassy in our capital city, Jakarta. However, weeks later, we received another letter telling us not to continue the process. In 1990, another letter came, this time saying that we were welcome once again to apply for a U.S. green card and that we had to schedule another interview with the American Embassy as soon as possible. We had four months to leave our country and move to the United States.

My husband went to America first, in April of 1991, to secure a place to stay and other necessary things for us. Within four months, I had to sell the house, furniture, appliances, books, and all our belongings to collect the money for the trip. Our currency value was very low, compared to the U.S. dollar at the time. One dollar equaled two thousand rupees back then. I joined my husband in America with my two little children on August 19, 1991.

I could not imagine what America would be like because I had never traveled abroad. I had only traveled within Indonesia. The main reasons for immigrating to the United States included having better opportunities, better quality of life, and a better future and education for my children. I had prepared for the difficulties of living in a new country with a different language than mine, as well as different culture and weather.

I flew from Indonesia to Hawaii and then continued to Los Angeles. At the beginning, I joined an Indonesian church and I met Indonesian people who became my friends. After a while, I thought about joining an American church to learn about the new culture and have more chances of practicing English. The majority of the church members in the American church are white. Although the church members are nice,

---

[13] Each year, Diversity Visa Program provides 50,000 immigrant visas through a lottery to people who come from countries that have sent less than 50,000 immigrants to the U.S. in the past five years. The State Department's National Visa Center holds the lottery every year, and chooses winners randomly from all qualified entries. Anyone selected under this lottery will be given the opportunity to apply for permanent residence and to bring his/her spouse and any unmarried children under the age of 21 to the U.S.

it is not easy to fit into this society and I have the feeling that they are not really my friends. I still feel like an outsider. It is not because they are unfriendly, but because of the language barrier. It seems awkward and uncomfortable to chat with them. Sometimes I experience cultural misunderstandings because I do not understand the jokes my American friends tell me.

Surprisingly, my daughter, who is very eloquent and fluent in English, has the same feeling that I do. We do not fit; we are not Americans, even though all the members of my family are U.S. citizens. My daughter questions her identity and feels like an outsider because of her ethnic background.

When I started to work at a school as a Special Education assistant, I felt a little bit better because my friends at work came from different ethnic backgrounds. I felt that we were in the same boat as we are not native English speakers, and because of having the same experiences as immigrants, we feel bonded as friends.

After about seventeen years living in this country, my English is still not perfect. I believe this contributes to the distance and difference between me and the society around me. However, I do not stop trying to overcome my limitations as an immigrant. I have to think as positively as possible rather than dwelling on negative thoughts. I have to move on and take whatever opportunities appear to improve myself as much as possible. This is a country of hope and opportunity for every immigrant. I always think of Martin Luther King Jr.'s speech "I have a dream." Rather than looking at the dark side of immigrant's life, I move on and welcome all future hope that I expect from this country.

Both of my children have received a very good education in prestigious universities in this country without paying a lot of money because of financial aid and scholarships, which would have been almost impossible to get had we not moved to America. My children were able to work since they were in high school, which enabled them to travel abroad and see many different countries. This is the beauty of living in America. My children would not have had these opportunities had we not come here. They would not have been able to see many parts of the world using their own money. I believe I was not wrong when I made the decision to move to America.

Life is full of positive and negative sides, mountains and valleys. It is not always bad being an immigrant. It depends on how we perceive life. There are many successful immigrants living in this country. I feel very lucky to be an immigrant, so my children will have a bright future.

From Mexico to California: A Teenager's Journey

—Víctor Zúñiga

We came from Mexico City. My family decided to immigrate to the United States because they were looking for better opportunities. I was twelve when my brother and I immigrated. My parents had come a year before us.

My mom had known someone in Mexico who had left to go to the United States. This friend was encouraging her to leave Mexico and go to California where there are more job opportunities and the possibility of having a better life than in Mexico. My mom decided to leave and she crossed the border with the assistance of some relatives who arranged some contacts at the border to help her cross. When she arrived, she stayed in her friend's apartment for a couple of months while she looked for a job and saved some money. My father joined her two months later. For my father, crossing the border was much more difficult. He had paid some people (*coyotes*) to guide him through the border and to take him to safety once in the United States. However, these *coyotes* abandoned my father in the desert once he crossed the border. My father was lost for five days in the desert; he kept on walking but didn't know where he was going. He had no water or food for five days and it was a miracle that he survived the dangers of the desert. Finally he was able to get in touch with my mother who went to pick him up and take him to their new life in Santa Barbara, California. When my father arrived, they had to move out of the friend's apartment. Luckily, they found another place to live. My father started working as a gardener and my mother continued working as a cleaning lady. They kept on saving money until they were ready to send for my brother and me to join them in California.

I didn't know how I was supposed to feel about coming to the United States. I had mixed feelings and contradictory emotions; there was anger, sadness, and happiness. I was angry with my parents for leaving me and my brother for a year with uncles and aunts who didn't really care about us. I used to consider these relatives family, but now I know that my only true family is my parents and my brother. I felt great sadness when we were boarding the plane from Mexico City to Tijuana since I realized it was probably going to be the last time I would see the place where I grew up. However, happiness came at last when I met with my parents for the first time in a year.

My trip to the United States was short. My brother and I took a plane to Tijuana, Mexico, and throughout the flight I started thinking about how my life was changing and how it was going to affect me in the future. This was the first time that I had been on a one-way journey. I knew that I wouldn't be going back and that this was not like a vacation, although I wanted to believe that it was. One of the first thoughts in my mind was that I would go back to Mexico. This idea is always in my mind and I can't ignore its existence. If I did, it would be like denying my own existence. From the airplane, everything below us looked simple and people were just little dots on the ground. No wonder people used to think the world was flat!

My brother and I arrived in Tijuana and then waited in a house thirty minutes away from the U.S. border. Tijuana was boring since we were not allowed to go out at any time, mainly for safety reasons. We were told that Tijuana is a dangerous place to live. The place where we stayed seemed to be under construction with everything out of order and in pieces. A woman whom I didn't know came to pick us up at ten in the morning the following day. My parents had contacted this person to help us cross the border by pretending that we were her sons. However, her real son was around five years older than me and around seven years older than my brother! The plan was for us to pretend to be asleep in her car while crossing the border. However, since this person had only one son, my brother and I had to cross the border separately at different times. I crossed the border first. I was scared and worried because I was leaving my younger brother behind in a strange place with people I had never seen before. I made it safely to the other side. Then, it was my brother's turn. The woman went back to Tijuana to pick up my brother and he crossed the border doing the same thing I had done before him: pretending to be her son and to be asleep in the car. When my brother crossed, we stayed at an ugly house in San Diego, California. I could not sleep because I had seen a rat and many cockroaches earlier that day. I even felt something moving on my head when I was trying to get some sleep! From San Diego, a friend of my parents drove my brother and me to the Los Angeles Greyhound bus station. My parents picked us up there and then took us to Santa Barbara. Since my parents had been living in the United States for a year already, they had managed to get jobs and a small apartment in a neighborhood close to a community college.

In Mexico, I knew everyone in the neighborhood where I was born. I lived close to my family, aunts, uncles, and cousins. Everyone spoke the same language and I used to play soccer every day. I left behind friends and family and I was sad about this. But now, I only miss the ones who actually cared about us.

When I left Mexico, I was in seventh grade doing well in Spanish as that is my first language. In Mexico, I was taking 15 classes in seventh grade and to be able to attend the middle school, I had to take an entrance exam. My classes varied from algebra, physics, and chemistry, to languages such as French and English. The English classes were helpful, but they were not enough to speak the language well when I came to the United States. With no surprise, my first day of school in the United States was horrible. The classes were a lot easier but I was laughed at because of my English. I learned to ignore racist jokes, given that even children of my own race would make them. I heard "wetback" and "beaner" so many times I learned to block these words out of my system. Most teachers and classmates were not at all helpful in my adjusting to the U.S. school system. Additionally, not knowing the language well made me feel like an idiot; it made me feel like I was inferior to everyone else.

While I was struggling with the language, my brother was making friends and getting a better grasp of the language. He was not struggling too much and the reason for this was that he had a friend, Jared. My brother met Jared at school. Jared had lots of patience and would help us with our "mocho" English (*mocho* means 'broken' in Mexico City's slang). He is the only person who never made fun of how we pronounced words. Jared is African American, a real brother. My parents unofficially adopted him and we are still friends. Aside from Jared, there was also a teacher in the middle school who helped me. I think she saw I was in need of help and lonely. She got me into a robotics and science club that was a little nerdy but I liked it. She told me that I would make it to college. However, I didn't believe her until I actually stepped into the university. She would sit with me and help me with my English homework. I would not speak in any of my classes because I was afraid of messing up, but eventually I had to and it was then that I had not one but many embarrassing moments. I would be so tangled in the language that I would just excuse myself and then keep quiet. I attended middle and high school in the United States. The school system is different from the one I was used to in Mexico and it is a lot easier here.

Currently, I am a sophomore at the university. I live close to campus in a rented room in a house. Whenever I can, I also work as a gardener in Santa Barbara with my father. I think I speak enough English to do well at the university. My Spanish speaking and writing skills are the same. Sometimes I do not remember words in either language and that is something I am trying to work on. Based on my current legal situation it is hard to know how my future in the United States will turn out, but I have dreams and hopes that things will get better and as long as I have these ideas in my mind I will continue my uncertain journey.

Worlds Apart

—Thuy Le

I am a spoiled Asian American who gets what I want from my parents. I have lived a mostly sheltered life full of wonders and possibilities. There has never been a time when I went hungry or had to risk my life to save another. All this was possible thanks to my parents, who risked their lives to escape Vietnam on a fishing boat in 1985.

For six days and seven nights, three men disguised as fishermen steered a fishing boat with 52 people hidden on the bottom of the boat. This was how my parents escaped to an island called Batawan, Philippines, the city where I was born. The people on the boat consisted of men, women (some pregnant), elderly, and children, all of whom had a slim chance of surviving. Not only did they have to endure the harsh conditions of the sea on the rickety boat not made for the high sea but they also had to watch out for marauders because this South China Sea abounded with notorious Thai pirates who robbed, raped, or killed their captives. My mother's side of the family had eight people. My father had only his brother whom he stowed secretly on the ship. Upon arriving in the Philippines, we were helped by friendly villagers. Our family was fortunate because we were recognized as refugees and were sponsored by the United States to come to America.

The fall of Saigon in 1975 left my family with nothing. Overnight, money became more worthless than rags. Complete poverty hit my family and there were no means of survival in Vietnam. My grandfather on my mother's side worked for the South Vietnamese Army as an aviator making a good income to support his seven children. But after the communist takeover, if he had been found, he would have been sent to the re-education camps to be imprisoned and killed. My father was young when he lost his father in the war and has always been poor. Shortly after the communist took over Vietnam, it appeared that no business could thrive and no human could survive as Vietnam faced famine and another war with Cambodia. For many people, the only way for survival was to escape by any means.

At the time, my parents were young lovers. They were around my age, about 22 years old. At the time of departure, my mom was already five months pregnant with me. They had been hiding the pregnancy before their departure. With everything that was going on, they could not break the news for fear that everyone would worry. Everybody was stressed and worried enough about everything else. My parents knew there was no way that the baby could survive in Vietnam without the help of family, and they could not stay in a land where medical help was impossible to find and food was scarce. They would have done and given anything to be together and raise a family. They put all their hopes for their baby's survival on this escape boat. During the whole trip, both were scared and feared for their lives in every waking hour. Everyone knew the trip would be dangerous and they might not make it either by being lost at sea, being caught, or being captured by pirates. My father would tell me that my mother would sit up and cry every night while she was on the boat. She feared that I would not even be born and felt guilty to give birth to a child during such a horrible time.

My grandfather Lam is a hardworking man. He worked in the South Vietnamese military for 15 years as an air force aviator. He served and defended the country he loved and never would have imagined that the country he would give his life for could imprison and kill him. He knew if he were to leave, he would never be able to come back home. Coming back would never be an option because he was a wanted man and no matter how much time passed, that would not change.

The passengers on the boat left behind everything they had worked for to start a new life in a foreign land without knowing whether they could return and see their families again. Life in Vietnam was gone and they were forced to start all over in a foreign country with no prior knowledge of the country's language. Only one thing was certain: if they stayed in Vietnam they would die, and risking everything and fleeing to another country was the only choice. Their families in Vietnam depended on their survival.

It took five months in the Philippines for my family to be granted admission to the United States. We were considered very lucky because we already had family members in the United States to sponsor us. Our family was divided; my grandparents went to Washington State, my aunts to Michigan, some to California, and my parents and I to Texas. No one wanted to split up, but with so many people we had to do so to speed up the settling process.

My family lived in Texas for three years before coming to our current residence of Rosemead, California. Coming to America was very difficult for my parents. Surviving in America proved to be another difficulty. They had no experience in any jobs that they could utilize in America and they had an extra mouth to feed. In Vietnam, my mother sold gasoline for boats during the nights and my father sold seashells. None of their experiences could be used to work in America without knowing the language. It was even harder because I was a very sick child who cried constantly and was not able to digest my mother's milk. When I did, I would vomit, and buying baby formula was far too expensive. They had no other choice but to feed me whole milk even though I was just six months old.

In Texas, my father found a job at a local bakery working the night shifts. He worked long hours; however, it was a hard struggle between putting food on the table and saving to move to California. He worked there until we could save enough money to go to California where his stepsister lived. Once arriving in California, my father worked with the family moving furniture. It was a livable income and we were able to rent a small shack behind the landlord's house. That place was run down and dirty. It was infested with big black cockroaches that bred in the empty pool.

Life seemed to be heading in a great direction for my parents. They started learning English from my father's nephews who were in high school. After about three years, my parents were able to move out and rent a four-bedroom house with three other roommates. There were a total of seven people living in that house. My father went to school, learned to be a handyman in household electronics, and started his own business. He would find used or abandoned electrical devices such as refrigerators, washers, and dryers, and repair them. The business was in our garage. As years went by, my father established a name for himself and soon had a steady customer base. His customers were all immigrants like us. Then my parents added two more members— my younger sister and younger brother—to our family.

While I was growing up, my parents never told me about their struggles and sacrifices. It was too difficult and hard to tell. Instead, they pampered me with all the things they could not afford as a child. They loved to buy me new toys and the cutest dresses. The welfare system of the U.S. government helped my parents to save and send money back home in Vietnam. Food stamps were one of the key components that made my parents successful in America.

However, life in America was never easy for my parents because they constantly had a fear of being deported back to Vietnam. They had documents to stay in the United States but they were not fully aware of the law so they always remained silent and passive. They always kept me inside the house and made me focus on my studies. Even when I had no homework to do, I had to always sit at my desk and read. I grew up somewhat alone without people in my age group to play with. Even when my sister Sara was born she had to be sent to my grandparents' house in Washington because my parents could not afford to stay home to watch her.

We finally became citizens after eight years. My parents could afford to buy their own home after 15 years. Since we moved to California we have lived in only one city, Rosemead. Along with the house, my father was able to buy two brand-new cars with monthly payments based on his good credit. I remember my father saying, "Finally my dreams have come true." His dream was to become a citizen, raise a family, and buy a house to pass down to his children.

It was not until my sophomore year of college when I took Asian American Studies courses that I realized how much my parents had struggled. Stories of their past came up every now and then, but I was never able to piece them together. I would be lying if I would say I understood what my parents went through 22 years ago. I can only understand a fraction of what they endured, and even that seems all right with them. I suppose that is the way they want it to be.

Communication between parents and children has been quite poor in my family. Positive words have never been exchanged between my parents and me. The connection between my parents and me is not that strong due to our generation gap. We at times do not understand each others' worlds. The generational conflict was the worst during my teenage years because my parents kept trying to restrict my activities within our home while I wanted to explore the outside world by joining clubs and playing sports like the other kids. It was hard for me to express my emotional feelings to my parents due to the language barrier between my parents and me and as a result, I became very rebellious. For my parents, they could not express how they felt in English, so they chose to discipline me through physical punishment and authoritarian control. To this day, I believe my parents' harsh discipline to be the main cause for my low self-esteem, my fear of failure, and never thinking I am good enough. These doubts I have about myself are always within me.

I am not sure if my parents and I can ever emotionally bond together, but I know that even though they may have treated me harshly, it was out of love. Through my experience, I came to understand that it is not easy for children of immigrants to become who they want to become. However, I strive to be myself no matter what my parents say because in the end it is my life and they should not hold me back. I believe that my being an independent person allowed me to explore different majors at the university and helped me develop into who I want to become. However, I also want my parents to understand that I appreciate their love and everything they have done.

Language barriers and cultural differences between people can definitely create invisible borders between them. Sometimes these barriers create tension, which results in negative images of others. In this sense, many first- and second-generation children are at a disadvantage both in and outside of their home and culture. That is why it is important for teachers to be sensitive toward each student's family background including the immigration history and language used at home. Knowing students' family migration history may provide teachers with crucial understanding about cultural and generational conflict and tension that the student might be experiencing. It will also help teachers to teach students to be sympathetic toward one another and have an open mind to learn new things from immigrant students. We need to be mindful of others' immigration experience and show sensitivity. Classrooms are a place where we can learn from each other and at the same time mature together.

From the "Rancho" to the Metropolis

—Lucia Castillo

My family migration to the United States involves three generations. The first generation is my grandparents who were the first to come to the United States seeking a better life. The second generation is my parents, who decided to come to the United States for a better opportunity for their family. Last, the third generation is my siblings and me. Some of the factors that brought us to the United States were the possibility of a better education, better government, and better job opportunities than our country could provide for us.

My grandmother Maria de Jesus Morales Ayala was the first one who came to the United States. She was born in a rural ranch called "Las Playas," a municipality of Tlazazalca, Michoacan, Mexico, on February 16, 1926. This was a small town where no one had access to an education. Unfortunately, my grandmother did not have the opportunity to be educated and prepare herself to succeed in life. Instead of learning to read and write, my grandmother was taught to feed the animals and to cook and wash the clothes by hand. For this reason, my grandmother faced difficulties here in the United States. Because her experiences were limited by working on a ranch, she had a difficult time going to a clinic in the United States and had to have an interpreter. Other difficulties my grandmother faced involved the language barrier. It was very hard for my grandmother to adapt to a place where English is the primary language and sometimes she had to use gestures and signs as a means of communication. In the 1940s she decided to come to Los Angeles, California, with her husband and some of her children. They all planned to work and make enough money to return to Mexico. One child was born in the United States at that time. She returned to Mexico and raised her children. Much later, she immigrated again in the year 2000—this time because she wanted to stay with her family, almost all of whom now lived in the United States.

The second family member to immigrate to the United States was my father Ruben Castillo Morales. He was born on the same rural ranch as my grandparents in Michoacan, Mexico, on June 8, 1956. He grew up doing agricultural jobs in the fields of Mexico planting corn, beans, and squash and picking the crops. The ranch was the perfect place for him because there is no pollution and that kind of life is more relaxing for him. He was also able to do his favorite job, which is agriculture, and he was able to work with cows, goats, pigs, chickens, and horses. However, my father realized that having this kind of life was not working for him in terms of money. Even though he was working very hard day by day in the fields, he was not able to make enough money to help his parents economically. As a result, my father came to the United States as an undocumented worker in 1976. He immigrated to Washington State and found work in the pear, apple, and strawberry farms of Washington. He felt compelled to come to the United States because he wanted to help his parents financially. In Mexico, even though he worked a lot, he did not get paid adequately for all the work he had done in the entire day. His family was poor and they had just one room for 12 children and the parents. They had only one bed; obviously all of them could not fit in the same bed, which means that some had to sleep on the floor. The floor was very uncomfortable and the fleas would bite them while they were sleeping.

My father first immigrated to Los Angeles and stayed with his older brother Manuel Castillo. Later, he worked in the fields of Washington State. My father immigrated alone to the United States. He traveled from "La sierra de Temecula," risking his life since he could have been killed by wild animals or attacked by "moyos," who are brutal bandits known to rob and kill immigrants. The reason my father came is because he was told that there was a lot of farm work in the United States. He thought that he would like this type of work since he had farming experience.

Likewise, my family and I immigrated from a rural hometown located in Michoacan, Mexico, in the year 2000. Initially we thought we would be here for just nine months to make some money so we could build a bigger house in Mexico, but we ended up staying. We decided to stay because we saw that a better future awaited us here. My mother, brother, and I obtained our U.S. residency through my father in the consulate of Ciudad Juarez, a border town near El Paso, Texas. The most important reason we stayed in the United States was because my little sister Monica was diagnosed with brain palsy at the age of one. In Mexico there are not many specialists for that type of disease and therefore we came also looking for the type of special medical care that my sister needed.

It was very hard for us to adjust to the United States when we came. In Michoacan I did not go to school because there were not many schools. Also, the mentality of most of the people in Michoacan, where I came from, is that girls are not supposed to go to school; they are supposed to stay home and help their mothers do house chores. My grandmother and my mother were taught the same thing. When I came here to the United States I was 15 years old and had gone only to elementary school. Nevertheless, the school workers placed me in high school because I was too old. It was very hard for me to transition into being in school because my mentality was different and because of the language barrier. I did not know how to write well in Spanish and I was forced to learn a new language since everyone speaks English. I feel more comfortable speaking Spanish than I do speaking English because English is my second language and I started learning it only after I was 15 years old. Even though I do not feel as comfortable speaking English than I do speaking Spanish, I am able to communicate with other people very well. Also, now I have the skills to write, read, speak, and understand English, and I feel happy because I am realizing that all the hard work to get here proved to be worthwhile after all.

Initially, I had a lot of trouble adjusting to the United States and so did my parents and brothers. The two main reasons for this were that we did not speak the language but also because Los Angeles seemed like such a big place compared to our little ranch where we came from. We all felt frustrated because we came from a small town to a huge metropolis, and people in Los Angeles have different values and mentality.

However, my family and I adjusted to the different type of living in the United States. We had to learn to survive and learn a new culture. After high school I decided to go to college because I realized that getting a good education was the only way to be able to help my sister Monica. I made the decision to apply to California State University, Northridge. Since I am the first one in my family seeking a college education, I decided to work very hard and become a role model for my siblings.

From the Korean Beverly Hills to the LA Ghetto

—Hye-Young Kwon

By my desk, gathering dust now, there is a small box of letters and pictures written by my friends from South Korea. Some cards were from my best friends, who could not stop sobbing as I departed from the airport. One card was written by a shy male classmate, who on the day before I left for the United States, called to me in the playground, handed me the card, and quickly ran off. In a letter from my best friend, which came in an envelope with pictures of gold leaves and yellow daisies just above my name in the right corner, she asked me to send her pictures of Brad Pitt and invite her to my house when I settled down. She also enclosed a clipping of my middle school class photo from the school newsletter.

These letters are now very old but I've kept them in my room ever since I arrived in the United States in March of 1994. I don't read them as often as I used to, but this small box has been my source of comfort and escape from the unfamiliar environment in the United States for quite a long time. I never thought I would open this box so frequently, yearning for the memorable moments I shared with my friends in Korea. After all, I was moving to Los Angeles, the very center of all the glitz and glamour of Hollywood. Overblown with optimism, my sister and I could not fall asleep during the 14-hour-long plane trip, even as our mother wept next to us. Perhaps, my mother foresaw the hurdles and hardships that were awaiting us. Maybe it was heartbreaking for her to leave some of her family members and friends behind. But we were too excited to figure out why our mom was crying.

My aunt, on my mother's side, was the first person in our family to immigrate to the United States. She came in 1975 as a nurse. I never had a chance to develop a relationship with my aunt because she left Korea before I was born. Nevertheless, she always sent us gifts at Christmastime. It became routine for my sister and me to wait in front of our house for the mailman to arrive with a big gift box during the Christmas season. We then went to school wearing new trendy clothes from America and pompously carrying new sets of crayons that would captivate my classmates. I often bragged about my aunt, who owned a beautiful house with a big swimming pool and a gorgeous garden with green trees. To my sister and me, America was a place where everyone owned a beautiful house with a swimming pool and a garden.

According to my mother, my aunt was the risk taker in her family and was a very pragmatic and ambitious woman. She graduated from a university that was well known for nurse training in Seoul—the capital of Korea—and quickly took advantage of the 1965 Immigration Act, which had a provision specifically designed to recruit professionals from overseas. My aunt later told me that she was not the only person to immigrate to the United States from her school. From early on, students who attended this particular university were planning on immigrating to the United

States and entering a medical career after they arrived. As part of the preparation for her journey to the States, my aunt studied English at an English language school where she met my uncle-in-law as he too was getting ready to enter the technology sector as a mechanic.

My aunt and uncle's story share similarities with other post-1965 immigrants from East Asia in the early 1970s. The occupational preference category of the 1965 Immigration Act, which initially allowed new waves of highly skilled professional Asians to enter the United States, opened the floodgate to new immigrants from Asia to enter through the next preference category of family reunification. After my aunt obtained a job as a nurse in the States and gained permanent resident status through employment sponsorship, she was able to gain U.S. citizenship five years later. She then sponsored her mother under the immediate family preference category of the 1965 Immigration Act. My grandmother waited less than a year to come to the States because under this law, spouses, minors, and parents of U.S. citizens were exempted from the quota. My mother and uncles, on the other hand, waited more than 10 years after my aunt obtained her U.S. citizenship. As they were siblings of a U.S. citizen, in family-based immigration they got last priority in the preference system, therefore having a longer waiting period than other immediate relatives.

For my parents, immigrating to the States was a last resort. Before migrating to the United States, my father had owned a relatively big business manufacturing accessories and exporting them overseas. His business, like the economy of South Korea in the 1980s and 1990s, was booming rapidly. By the time I entered elementary school, my father's business flourished and our family had a stable life in the core of Seoul, Gang Nam, a place Koreans called "the Beverly Hills of Korea." Living in such a neighborhood denoted an upper-middle-class background, and even as an elementary school student, I had a private tutor helping me with my homework and a computer teacher who came to my house every week.

My life after school was very busy. I went from one private lesson to the other learning art, piano, and math. When I entered middle school, the competition was extremely fierce and more students were enrolling in private programs around the city to enhance their academic skills. Parents who could not provide such private education for their children were frowned upon, at least in the neighborhood I lived in. One day, I woke up in the middle of the night and overheard my parents arguing. My mother yelled, "What about the kids? There is no way for them to go to college in Korea if they have to move to another city. How are you going to pay for the private schools that they are attending now? There is really no way for them to go to college. No way!" She slammed the door really hard and cried in the dark. I later found out that my father's business was in jeopardy. My father indeed had benefited significantly from South Korea's export-oriented industrialization process; it had developed rapidly under the South Korean leadership who supported export-driven industrialism that was heavily dependent on the labor-intensive manufacturing industries. South Korea as a nation was being modernized very rapidly but there were consequences to its swift economic development. When recession hit Korea in the 1990s, smaller size enterprises, like my dad's business, had a hard time surviving the economic downturn. The aura of capitalism permeated the whole country: class inequality mushroomed all over the country while the fierce economic competition and population pressure pushed many well-educated South Koreans to seek a more stable life outside of the country.

On December 25, 1993, our family had dinner at a nearby restaurant to celebrate Christmas. The streets were very crowded and busy. The weather was extremely cold. The neon lights were bright, and there were several events occurring in the streets. When we got to the restaurant, my parents looked at each other, and my mother asked, "Did you ever think about living in the United States?" I was surprised and wasn't quite sure how to answer her question because I had never thought of moving to the United States. It was all too much to consider, but reflecting back at the moment, I was secretly happy to escape the "examination hell," a harsh regime of endless cramming and rote memorization of facts that I had to go through in order to enter the prestigious college in South Korea. I recalled the pictures of my aunt's house when I told my mother that it would be very exciting to move to the United States.

I had no idea that this was going to be the last Christmas that I was to spend in Korea. After that night, everything moved really quickly and three months later, I had to say goodbye to my friends and leave Korea. When I asked my mother why she did not tell us about the possibility of moving to the United States earlier so my sister and I could prepare for our journey, she simply said, "It was because your father and I were unsure whether we could immigrate to the United States. The wait was too long and we were told that sometimes immigration petitions get rejected at the last minute." Apparently, my parents were very anxious because my father's business was about to close down. They nervously inquired about their waiting status and when they finally heard from the South Korean consulate that we could immigrate to the United States, they were relieved. It was perfect timing and my parents did not hesitate to make rather a big decision.

Nevertheless, there was a clear difference between my aunt's migration path and my family's journey to the United States. While my aunt and uncle-in-law had the professional skills the United States desired, my parents did not have the training nor skills they needed to earn a decent income. My aunt clearly saw an economic opportunity because the United States provided greater financial rewards for her professional training in comparison to what was available for her in South Korea. This does not mean that my aunt actually experienced the comfortable life that she envisioned. Upon arriving in the United States, she realized that it was extremely difficult to transform her education into a desirable profession or position. As a result, she started from the bottom up as a nurse. She worked in hospitals that other white nurses did not want to go to and worked night shifts to maintain her employment.

However, as immigrants who took advantage of the family unification category of the immigration law—not the occupational preference system—we were in a different boat. Not only did my parents not have training as professionals or highly skilled workers but they also did not have the economic means to start a small business in the United States, like many other Korean immigrants did. As a result of filing bankruptcy in South Korea, my father did not have enough financial means to even rent a home of his own. Thus, we had to stay at my grandmother's one-bedroom apartment in Koreatown after arriving in the United States. The neighborhood in Koreatown and the school that I attended were not the America that I dreamed of. I could not find a single house that resembled my aunt's house in the picture. Instead, what I witnessed was a third world neighborhood within the richest nation in the world. My next-door neighbor had five children in a one-bedroom apartment. The first phrase I learned in English was, "I am sorry. I don't have money" because there were so many homeless people in my neighborhood asking for money.

My uncle on my mother's side, who was barely able to communicate with his broken English, took my sister and me to a nearby middle school where the majority of students were qualified to receive free lunch at the school. Every day at lunch, I stood in the long "free lunch" line despite the fact that the "cash" line was almost empty and moved very quickly. I later found out that I was tracked into what students then called the "FOB" (fresh off the boat) track where the majority of students were English learners. Due to a large population of Latino students in my school and particularly in my track, I learned Spanish before I learned English. I remember going around the campus saying, "Hola, como estas? Amigo!" It is not surprising because I had to sit in a classroom with Spanish speakers and a bilingual teacher's assistant who constantly translated what the teacher was saying into Spanish. To me, both Spanish and English were foreign languages that I could not possibly understand. I could not tell one from the other. Everyday, I sat in my ESL class and drew pictures in my notebook and wrote letters to my friends in Korea telling them how frustrated I was and how I missed cracking jokes with them, playing soccer with them after class, and getting ready for the yearly singing contest.

One day, tears spilled from my eyes and dropped onto the pages of my English book as I wrote a letter to my best friend in Korea. I quickly got a pass to go to the restroom, sat on the toilet, and cried out loud. I missed my teachers in Korea, friends, and the friendly and familiar surroundings I had enjoyed. I was the popular kid in South Korea, I thought. I was a leader in the classroom, a teachers' pet, and was told that I was very capable. But my American teachers constantly reminded me of the bleakness of my life: Ha-yung quan? How come you are not good at math? I thought Asian kids are good at math. I did not know how to answer these kinds of questions. The truth was I never liked math and always had a private math tutor. I kept quiet whenever people asked me such questions and merely smiled back at them. Behind my agreeable appearance, however, lingered a sense of disenchantment.

Looking back, my journey to America and American life as a new immigrant became a catalyst for my search to better understand and resolve the social issues that deprive immigrants from their dignity, basic freedoms, and common respect. Though each individual's journey and experience in the United States is unique, there are many similarities. Deceived by the alluring scenes in media production and commercialization, many immigrants often embrace the idea of America as a country of freedom, opportunity, and wealth. Unlike their expectations, many immigrants feel powerless when they encounter social forces stemming from racism and social stratification. However, many hold on to their dreams with dignity and uphold their determination to survive.

As a teacher, I strive to hear the stories of the American journey from other immigrants, especially their life experiences that made them feel powerless and invisible. It is a constant struggle and I bear a responsibility to shape a safe community within the classroom. But teaching is a community project and I hope to hear the voices of and be the voice for the "fresh off the boat" girl hiding in the school bathroom, for the frustrated first-generation fathers, for the desperate mothers, and for the countless other immigrants missing from the common discourse.

A Story of Intergenerational Migration

—Yesenia A. Sánchez

Because economic conditions in Mexico were not as good as they were in the United States, my grandfather Roberto came to this country as a Bracero during the late 1950s, and again in the 1960s. My father, Alfredo Sanchez, at the age of 22 also decided to come to California to join his uncle. Since he did not have the funds or time to apply for legal entry, he crossed the border illegally. After working here for a few years, he went back to Aguascalientes, Mexico and married my mother, Ofelia Flores. After their marriage, in June 1981, they migrated to the United States legally with a valid passport and visa. During this time in the United States they had three children, my brothers Miguel, Luis, and Alfredo. Then in 1984, after my brother Alfredo was born, both my parents decided to go back to Aguascalientes, Mexico, and bought a house with their savings. They thought that now that they had funds to build their own home, life would be better in Mexico. However, in less than one year, they learned that it was still an economic struggle to make a decent living in Mexico and in 1985 they opted to come back to the United States with valid passports and visas, and my brothers had their birth certificates. At the border, for no apparent reason, an immigration officer denied entry to my parents and my brothers, and he took away my parents' visas and passports. The officer told my parents that the children were not his responsibility and that it was not his problem what they decided to do. My parents had to find a way to cross the border with my three brothers: Miguel, age three; Luis, age two; and Alfredo, age one. They crossed the border at Tijuana with the help of a *coyote* in October 1985. They had to cross the desert, my dad carrying two of my brothers, and my mom the other. Even after they crossed the desert, their journey was not finished because they still had to travel on a double-pack trailer hidden under boxes. Once they crossed the border, the *coyote* took them to a house in the city of El Cajon, California, to rest for one night. The next day another *coyote* brought all of the people from the first *coyote* to Escondido, and then to Santa Ana, and then to Los Angeles, where they finally arrived at my aunt's house. A year later, I was born.

When I was six months old, my parents decided to leave the United States again and go back to Mexico. The reason they went back this time is because my younger brother had asthma and the doctors told my parents that the Los Angeles smog was not good for him. Later, my parents tried to come back to the United States (to work and make more money to complete the construction of their home) before my mom gave birth to my sister Sonia; and even though they tried to come with a visa and our birth certificates, the immigration officer at the border did not let us come into the country. So my younger sister was born in Aguascalientes, Mexico, and my brothers, my sister, and I attended school in Aguascalientes. We had to be registered as Mexican citizens, so my parents registered my three brothers and myself as Mexicans born in Mesillas Tepezala. Mesillas Tepezala is a little ranch that belongs to the state of Aguascalientes, Mexico. I attended school in Mexico up to the fifth grade, and then when I was 10, my parents decided to come back to the United States. This time, we were supposedly coming just for a vacation, but my father was offered a job and we stayed. So my brothers, my sister, and I had to leave school, friends, and family behind. Luckily we left school during the summer vacation. I can rarely recall those days, but I can remember that I was sad because we did not get to go to the beach during the summer of 1997. My family had a tradition of going to the beach during summer vacation, and every year we went to a different beach.

Our final journey started in August 1997 when my dad made a promise to give us a better life. My brothers Miguel, Luis, Alfredo, and I had our birth certificates from the United States. My parents and my sister had their visas and passports. We got on a plane in Aguascalientes that took us to Tijuana where my uncle Pedro and my cousin Raul picked us up at the airport. My brothers and I crossed the border with my uncle, and while waiting to cross the border, I remember the fear I had inside because my parents and my sister had to cross the border on a bus. I was scared because I did not know what to say when the officers were interrogating us. The immigration officers did not believe that we were U.S. citizens because my brother Luis had an identification card of one of his friends from school in Mexico. The officers took my uncle Pedro to an office far away from our sight. My brothers, my cousin, and I were crying because we did not know what was going on with my uncle. The officers were threatening us by telling us that they were going to put my uncle and my brother Luis in jail if we did not tell them the truth, but we were not lying because the five of us are U.S. citizens, and my uncle is a legal resident of California. That day was one of the most horrifying in my life because I have never felt so threatened. Finally, the officers let my uncle out of the office, and we were able to conclude our journey to Los Angeles. We still had to go home with no news from my parents. After two days of waiting, my parents and my sister were able to come to the United States legally. Luckily, we were together after a day of fear with immigration and started our life in California.

My aunt Martha helped us a lot by letting us stay at her house for about a year. My dad called people whom he knew when he had previously lived and worked in California. My brothers, my sister, and I started school right away. I was enrolled in Bethune Middle School, in the city of Los Angeles. We did not attend regular classes right away because we had to attend special classes to prepare us to take a test for our placement. I don't remember my first day at school, but I do remember specific moments. There were both positive and negative moments in middle school. I can recall a security guard during lunchtime telling my brother to tuck in his shirt, but we could not understand what he was trying to tell us. It seemed that we could only understand body language because the security guard was putting his hand inside and outside his pants. We were enrolled in ESL classes for two years with Mr. Palacios who was from Belize. Other than the ESL class, the rest of the classes were taught in English. The first three years were difficult for us in school, and all we could think of was going back to Mexico. It was hard because we did not know the language spoken in school. Some teachers in middle school were helpful because they spoke Spanish, which made it easier for us. I graduated from Bethune Middle school in 2000 and attended John C. Fremont High School along with most of my friends from middle school. I started to speak English in my freshman year of high school. I was able to understand basic words, but I was unable to maintain a conversation because my mouth felt like it would crumble. My junior year was so much different from freshman and sophomore years, and the years in middle school. I cannot remember anyone helping me to learn the language, and the only way was to confront the language alone. My mom did not speak a word of English, and my dad did but he never taught us. I think he never taught us because he was afraid we would have his accent, so we just had to learn the language by ourselves. During my junior year, I had a drama class and I had to do a play about a mother who was 32 years old and dressed as a 20-year-old. One of the girls in the play noticed my pronunciation of the word "thirty." I would pronounce it with an accent, and Cristina helped me to pronounce it without an accent. After that play, I was able to go to Cristina and ask for help with the pronunciation of other words.

Some of the most painful memories that I have are the times when I took the high school exit exam. I did not do as well on the exit exam as many of the students who graduated in 2004. Before graduation I took the placement test for math and English, and based on the scores I earned, I had to take remedial courses in college. I graduated from high school on the Honor Roll and with a grade point average of 3.5, and with diplomas from my foreign language class. I decided to attend California State University, Northridge, and I am now an undergraduate at this university. I am almost finished with school and looking forward to getting my master's degree once I graduate. I can now say that I speak the English language though not at a high level of academic English. I am still learning, especially new vocabulary words. At this time of my life, my English proficiency is good enough to defend myself verbally at school and work and to have casual conversations with educated individuals. I can proudly say that I am able to maintain a conversation with a professor at a college and my mouth will not crumble any more. My native language is part of my life and I do speak the language well, but when it comes to writing, I fail because I do not recognize the locations of accent marks. I am definitely looking forward to taking classes to improve my Spanish writing.

Teachers are role models for students, so if the teachers fail, the students will also fail. It will be important for teachers to understand the feeling of a child who cannot communicate with others, including the teacher. How is it going to be possible for the student to bring homework to class if the students and the parents do not understand what the teacher is asking for? I think that teachers should be more understanding and sensitive when it comes to a second language learner student. If the teacher speaks some of the language of the student, the struggle of not speaking English will be less difficult. My major is liberal studies, and I am going to be a teacher. What I would do is to try to incorporate the students' culture and language in the class, letting them know that their native language and culture are important to me as they are to them. I believe that teachers can set the tone to facilitate a learning environment by demonstrating their understanding of students' immigrant backgrounds and their cultures and languages. I firmly believe that the student's future is in the hand of the teacher.

Escaping Khmer Rouge

—James Van

My family was one of the Khmer Rouge refugees who fled the country to seek asylum when their country was in turmoil. The refugees who were lucky enough to come to America were hoping for better opportunities, financial wealth, and simply a brighter future for their families and themselves. My parents were the first of our generation to arrive in the United States. They came to a new place where they had no clue of what to expect. My parents had to deal with the changes from Cambodia to the United States because there was no going back to what they were used to in their country.

My family did not have anyone to turn to for help or advice. They only had each other, but that was enough to get by. From my father's side of the family, my grandmother died during the rough times of the Khmer Rouge from starvation, emotional anguish, and stress. Grandfather, on the other hand, was lucky and strong enough to survive the horror of the Khmer Rouge and is still living in Cambodia. None of my father's siblings were fortunate enough to make it out of Cambodia. As for my mother's side of the family, only the grandmother and my two cousins were able to escape Cambodia alive along with my parents. Sadly, grandpa died of extreme physical exhaustion and intense grief of having to lose his family and everything he had ever worked hard for. My aunt and her husband were placed in different labor camps when the Khmer Rouge separated them according to age, height, sex, level of education, and so on. In the camps, they were probably tortured to death by the Khmer Rouge military under Pol Pot's orders. After more than 30 years have passed without any sign of them, my mother finally has given up hope of being reunited with her sister some day.

Both my mother and father were born in a small province in Cambodia, called Bontong, in the 1950s. Bontong is where they met in school and eventually married. Soon after marriage, my mother was pregnant with their first child in 1973. With a baby on its way, my father decided to move south to Battambang, Cambodia, to look for a better living and a brighter future for himself and his family. It was the first time my parents moved out of their parents' home to start a new life on their own. Their first child was born soon after they moved to a new city that they thought would be their new home. They were excited to start a new family independent from their parents. They would have never imagined that political change and ensuing turmoil in their country would shatter their dreams. Just two years after they settled down in Battambang, the Khmer Rouge declared Kampuchea a communist country governed by Pol Pot as the prime minister.

In July 1975, the Khmer Rouge had taken complete control of Battambang, Cambodia. The people of Cambodia were forced out of their homes and relocated into camps where they were put to work almost as slaves. Private businesses and personal properties were turned over to the Khmer Rouge army. Pol Pot was the head of operations for the Khmer Rouge. Pol Pot must have killed 1.3 to 2 million people, wiping out almost a quarter of the country's population. Pol Pot's intention was to purify the people of Cambodia returning the country to a primitive agricultural society. His excuse for the mass murders was to eliminate people who would become obstacles to the great new way of life.

My mother had been separated from my father because they were sent to different camps. My father was forced to work in the fields with the rest of the men while my mother was in another campsite nursing her young. Many weeks passed and my parents were still separated. Mother was afraid that she might never see her husband again. Luckily, my father was able to sneak out of his campsite at night and found my mother. Thousands of people were killed daily and everyone was praying that they were not the next ones to die. Countless tragic events took place during the Pol Pot regime in Cambodia.

It was 1979 when the ruthless rule of the Khmer Rouge reached its ending. Vietnam came to Cambodia's aid. Apparently a deal had gone sour between the ambassador of Vietnam and Pol Pot. Khmer Rouge refugees fled the scene trying to escape from the torturous camps, cities, and the country if possible. This was the time when my family made a run to Vietnam from Battambang, Cambodia. That life or death decision changed their lives forever. Father, mother, children, aunts, uncles, grandpa, grandma, and some friends hitched a ride together in cattle-carriers for a small piece of gold and a few valuables. They had to move discreetly along the dangerous trails, avoiding the Khmer Rouge seeking for runaway slaves. After the long, exhausting trip to the border of Vietnam, they came to find out that Vietnam didn't want any Cambodian refugees.

With their hope of escape lost, there was nothing to do but to run back to where they were originally from, Bongtong. That part of the country was not yet under the authority of the Khmer Rouge. Grandma and grandpa were still there in Bongtong City, so my parents headed back. When they got back to Bongtong, they packed their bags and went east heading for Thailand. Then from Thailand, they traveled to Indonesia by boat. And from Indonesia they flew to Singapore, where the U.S. planes were there ready to transport refugees to the States. I guess the United States felt that they were responsible for the bombing in Cambodia and recruiting the Hmongs to help fight the communists in Vietnam. I assume that is the reason the United States decided to intervene and helped rescue some of the refugees from Cambodia.

For most immigrants and refugees, the reasons for coming to the United States are to look for a better future and opportunities for the next generations to come. People don't just decide to leave behind their homelands with everything and move to another place if they are doing well in their country. Not only did my parents feel their lives were in danger but my brother also had a serious infection in his eye and needed surgery to correct his vision. My parents figured with the advanced technology that the United States has, they would try their luck here.

I was born in California in 1985. While growing up, I was fortunate to be able to experience and enjoy all the great aspects of American life. As a child I didn't really understand the hardships my parents had endured living in Cambodia, but as I am older now I appreciate all they have done to offer a better life for the family.

They came here with nothing and had to find a source of income to keep the family together. They realized that the new country is built on capitalist ideology and is not a communist society like Cambodia during the Khmer Rouge. My family had to adapt to the American lifestyle. My mother says that she was just glad to be alive and didn't mind where they were living as long as we were all together.

After living in Chinatown, Los Angeles, until I was two or three years old, my father moved us to Lincoln Heights, Los Angeles. It was still a typical urban ghetto but my father felt that we needed to move out of Chinatown and into a house which was roomier for seven of us to live more comfortably. My brothers and I grew up in the city of Los Angeles, California. Lincoln Heights was an old city with people of different backgrounds and cultures. It was predominantly Hispanic, but we got along with our neighbors and friends in school just fine. We all went to the same kindergarten and grade school until it was time for middle school, then we parted ways. Some of my brothers went to middle school in Los Angeles and one of my brothers and I went to Mount Gleason, a middle school in the Valley. Then, I finished high school in the Valley at Verdugo Hills High School. After finishing high school, I had decent enough grades to attend college. I followed my brother's footsteps in coming to California State University, Northridge. Thanks to my parents' motivation and support, I got to where I am today.

My family's immigration experience has influenced me to become a better person by having great morals and standards. I try not to take anything for granted in life because I believe that everything has a purpose. My family's motivation and determination to struggle to make it out alive of Pol Pot's killing fields has affected me extremely. Their story has an unbelievable outcome and I am grateful for everything they have provided me, especially the moral support that I needed.

I consider myself to be an Asian American and proud of it. I love my culture and family values. I respect the fact that we are Khmer Rouge refugees who have migrated to the United States. I am thankful that my parents came to America to live a life that Cambodia could not offer us. My parents' hardship and struggles have brought a promising future to my life in this new world and I will be forever grateful for that.

Though I was lucky to have my older brothers to help me, other children of immigrant parents are likely to struggle with education more than nonimmigrant children because they do not have many resources to help them with their studies. Immigrant parents may be unable to help their children with their education because they were not educated in America themselves. Moreover, poor immigrant parents are most likely working long hours to make ends meet, leaving them very little to no time to spend with their children. Without full support and supervision by their parents, some immigrant children might experience feelings of loneliness, helplessness, and lack of direction and this may lead these children to lose focus on academic achievement. Teachers should pay extra attention to these children with immigration backgrounds by encouraging them to stay focused and motivated to pursue a successful education. After-school tutoring and mentoring for these kids will help guide and give these students the confidence they need to achieve their academic goals.

Section 2

LEARNING ENGLISH

Introduction to the Section by Ana Sánchez Muñoz

Ethnic Minority Children in U.S. and California Schools

The United States is a very diverse country culturally and linguistically. According to the U.S. Census Bureau (2000), approximately 47 million of the population (roughly 18%) five years of age and older speak a language other than English as their home language.[1] Most of the children of non-English-speaking families attend U.S. schools and are classified as English Language Learners (ELLs). In fact, 10.5% of the students enrolled in grades K–12 in U.S. public schools are ELLs. The Hispanic/Latino population is the largest segment of the ELL population in the country, with Spanish as the most spoken language in the United States after English.[2]

California is one of the most diverse states in the nation and this is reflected in the high numbers of minority children enrolled in public schools. More than 35.5% of the California population is classified as Hispanic/Latino.[3] Therefore, it is not surprising that the majority of the children enrolled in K–12 in California are Hispanic, who make up more than 48% of the student population, outnumbering white students by more than 18%. California also has the largest percentage of Asian residents in the continental United States (12.3%).[4] The population of Asian descent is very diverse reflecting many countries of origin and an even larger number of home languages. Of these, the most frequently spoken languages among California ELL Asian students are Vietnamese (2.2%), Filipino (1.4%), Cantonese (1.4%), Hmong (1.3%), and Korean (1.1%).[5]

The implications of these revealing numbers are clear: teachers in the United States in general and especially in California must be prepared to work with students who are acquiring English as a second or third or fourth language.

Language Acquisition: Theories and Implications

Understanding the challenges that ELL students face requires a knowledge of how one acquires language. Much of the research on second language acquisition builds on the different theories that try to explain how humans acquire their native language. The main categories of language acquisition theories include (1) theories

---

[1] U.S. Census Bureau Summary Tables on Language Use and English Ability, January 16, 2008, http://www.census.gov/population/www/cen2000/phc-t20.html.

[2] Ibid.

[3] U.S. Census Bureau State and County Quick Facts (California), January 16, 2008, http://www.census.gov/Press-Release/www/releases/archives/population/004083.html.

[4] State of California Education Profile, Fiscal Year 2006–07, December 17, 2007, http://www.ed-data.k12.ca.us/.

[5] Ibid.

derived from behaviorism, which propose that language is acquired through a process of habit formation; (2) nativist theories arguing that children are born with an innate ability to acquire language; and (3) sociocultural theories that emphasize the interaction between the individual and the culture and the pivotal role that language plays as a means for cultural transmission and communication.

Behaviorism, nativist theory, and interactionist theory explain language development differently; each contributes unique perspectives on this process. Despite the great contributions of these methodologies and theories, the question still remains of what is the best way to teach a second language to an increasing number of ELLs. However, the most likely answer is that there is no single best way to learn a language; rather, a combination of theories and methods becomes necessary to address the complexity of factors that influence language acquisition. As our classrooms continue to grow in cultural and linguistic diversity, teachers must face new challenges. Schools respond with a variety of programs that use differing strategies to teach English. Some of the instructional models for English language learners are discussed below.

Current Instructional Models and Programs: Do These Meet the Specific Needs of Our Immigrant Children?

There are diverse programs that have been specifically designed to address the large number of students that come to U.S. schools with little or no knowledge of English. According to Huerta-Macías (2005),[6] the most common educational models include English as a Second Language (ESL), Two-Way Immersion Programs, and Sheltered Instruction Programs.

Bilingual education in the United States has been primarily transitional in nature.[7] The idea underlying bilingual education programs is to offer content area instruction in the native language while students are developing English as a second (or other) language. However, very few of the bilingual programs in this country have bilingualism or biliteracy as a goal. The result has often led to replacement of the first language for academic purposes, eventually leading to heritage language attrition or even loss.

ESL programs are designed to provide English language instruction to ethnic minority students to help them develop the necessary skills in English for successful academic work. There are different types of ESL programs. Some models provide ESL pull-out classes, which involve "pulling-out" students from one or more classrooms or grade

---

[6] A. G. Huerta-Macias, *Working with English Language Learners* (Dubuque, IA: Kendall/Hunt, 2005).
[7] Ibid., 10.

levels to attend special intensive language classes for part of each day. On the other hand, push-in programs provide direct instruction to ELLs in the mainstream classroom. All ESL programs focus only on English language development and aim to mainstream students into English-only classrooms in the least amount of time possible. The goal is not for children to acquire English while, at the same time, they develop literacy skills in their first language (additive bilingualism). Rather, the outcome of transitional programs is the replacement of the native language by English in all academic areas (subtractive bilingualism).

Two-way immersion programs (TWI) are a form of dual language program and integrate language minority students (English learners) and language majority students (English speakers). The main difference between TWI and transitional bilingual education is that the former promotes additive bilingualism by developing literacy in the first language as well as proficiency in the second language. Research shows that TWI programs are better since they promote quality instruction in both languages and create positive cross-cultural attitudes for all students.

Sheltered instruction is an instructional approach that integrates subject matter and English language development. The primary aim is to facilitate instruction for ELLs in content area teaching. There are different models of sheltered instruction. Recent models emphasize the need to develop not only English language and academic skills but also sociocultural awareness among ELLs.[8] Even though some models of sheltered instruction have proven effective in addressing the academic needs of ELLs (e.g., the SIOP Model),[9] the program does not specifically address the heritage languages of students as bilingualism or biliteracy is not the primary goal.

Linguistic research shows that as students acquire a variety of registers in English, their home language suffers attrition, being relegated to very casual registers; eventually, the first language may be lost due to the restriction of domains of use.[10] Losing fluency in the home language often leads to linguistic insecurity and inhibition that directly interferes with the language development process (cf. Valdés 2001;[11] Villa 1996[12]).

---

[8] Ibid., 12.

[9] J. Echevarria, M. Vogt, and D. J. Short, *Making Content Comprehensible for English Learners: The SIOP Model* (2nd ed.) (Boston, MA: Pearson Education, 2004).

[10] A. Sánchez-Muñoz, "Style Variation in Spanish as a Heritage Language: A Study of Discourse Particles in Academic and Non-Academic Registers," in *Spanish in Contact: Policy, Social and Linguistic Inquiries*, ed. K. Potowski and R. Cameron, 153—171 (Amsterdam: John Benjamins, 2007).

[11] G. Valdés, "Heritage Language Students: Profiles and Possibilities," in *Heritage languages in America: Preserving a National Resource*, ed. J. K. Peyton, D. Ranard, and S. McGinnis, 37—77 (Washington, DC: Delta Systems and Center for Applied Linguistics, 2001).

[12] Villa, D. "Choosing a 'Standard' Variety of Spanish for the Instruction of Native Spanish Speakers in the U.S.," *Foreign Language Annals* 29 (1996): 191—200.

The Case of Ethnic Minority Education in California: From Bilingualism to English-Only

As we mentioned earlier, California has one of the most diverse student populations in the country. According to the California Department of Education, 25% of the students enrolled in K–12 public schools were classified as ELLs. Thus, the development and implementation of adequate education for language minority students is especially crucial in this state. On June 2, 1998, the state adopted Proposition 227, which essentially outlaws nearly all primary language instruction. Before this, California had a variety of education models of instruction for language minority students; these included dual immersion and late-exit transitional bilingual education programs that were offering promising results in academic achievement and language learning for ELLs. The passage of Proposition 227 was a major setback for bilingual education and prompted other states to follow the trend of English-only initiatives (e.g., Arizona, 2000).

The current anti-bilingual education movement is taking hold in many states across the nation and has negative consequences that not only affect our immigrant children now but also jeopardize the quality of education in the United States for future generations. Ample research has shown that instruction in the native language will not prevent or retard the acquisition of English. Additionally, literacy in the first language has been proven to help students acquire academic skills in a second language.[13] Bilingualism should be considered a valuable skill for anyone and not a drawback. In a global world where multilingualism is the norm rather than the exception, the U.S. English-only movement is out of sync with the current times and endangers the ability of our children to compete in a global economy.

The stories that follow describe the experiences of seven ELL children in the California's public school system. The authors, now adults, recall their school years and reflect on their journey to master the English language needed to succeed in their host society. Their stories speak of their difficulties and frustrations as they struggled to adjust to American schools. Some of the authors, such as Mayra, Alma, and Kylie, recall the fear that they felt their first day in a U.S. school and the frustration of not being able to understand anything of what was going on around them. They felt insecure, they felt lonely, and they feared being ridiculed if they tried to speak English, as Danthuy and Amy tell us. Yet these stories also express the joy of overcoming those obstacles in their pursuit of becoming educated and successful citizens. Some authors not only succeed but also excel in school; for example, Carlos and Mayra were able to graduate with honors and pursue higher education. Authors like Carlos became quickly and comfortably adjusted to the new environment and to U.S. school culture.

---

[13] S. Krashen, *Under Attack: The Case against Bilingual Education* (Burlingame, CA: Language Education Associates, 1996).

However, for most of them, the adjustment was slow and painful at times. Many struggled throughout their school years trying hard to overcome the language barrier so they could compete academically with mainstream students. The struggle with English is not exclusive to immigrant children but also affects U.S. born minority children. For example, Seaksan's story speaks volumes about the inadequacy of ESL programs and reminds us of our responsibility as educators not to forsake our U.S. born minority students. Seaksan's story of his school's failure to educate him contrasts sharply with Carlos's story of school success. Paradoxically, Seaksan was born in the United States whereas Carlos is a recent immigrant. This example defies preconceived ideas about immigrants and illustrates the variety of experiences that our Asian American and Latino students face in this country. Our hope is that you may find these stories helpful in understanding the linguistic challenges as well as the needs and feelings of immigrant children.

Bibliography

Echevarria, Jana, Vogt, Mary Ellen, and Short, Deborah J. *Making Content Comprehensible for English Learners: The Siop Model*. 2nd ed. Boston, MA: Pearson Education, 2004.

Huerta-Macias, Ana G. *Working with English Language Learners*. Dubuque, IA: Kendall/Hunt, 2005.

Krashen, Stephen. *Under Attack: The Case against Bilingual Education*. Burlingame, CA: Language Education Associates, 1996.

Sánchez-Muñoz, Ana. "Style Variation in Spanish as a Heritage Language: A Study of Discourse Particles in Academic and Non-Academic Registers." In *Spanish in Contact: Policy, Social and Linguistic Inquiries*, edited by Kim Potowski and Richard Cameron, 153–71. Amsterdam: John Benjamins, 2007.

Valdés, Guadalupe. "Heritage Language Students: Profiles and Possibilities." In *Heritage Languages in America: Preserving a National Resource*, edited by Donald A. Ranard, Joy Kreeft Peyton, and Scott McGinnis, 37–77. McHenry, IL: Center for Applied Linguistics and Delta Publishing, 2001.

Villa, Daniel. "Choosing a 'Standard' Variety of Spanish for the Instruction of Native Spanish Speakers in the U.S." *Foreign Language Annals* 29 (1996): 191–200.

Mute and Invisible

—Mayra Nunez

How do I begin telling my story? Where do I start? Should I tell you that I was mute for about three years? Or should I say that my desperation took me to a level of insecurity never before faced? Or should I tell you that I found myself being someone who was not me?

I was born in Los Angeles but when I was four years old my parents decided to move back to Mexico. I am not sure why we moved back, but my dad said it was because of lack of money. When I was 15, my parents decided to move back to the United States. I was not sure again why, but my dad said that it was for a better future and more money. At the beginning, I was excited. I wanted to come to this country. I never thought it was going to be so hard.

I remember my first day of class. I was the new, invisible girl at John Marshall High School. I was used to my old high school in Mexico that had about 90 students and nuns walking all around. Here, I found a school with almost 3,000 students and police watching over us. I was afraid. My sister left me at the entrance of the school and said, "Estaras bien" (You will be all right). My heart was beating; I think it was getting ready for the hardest time of my life. It was getting ready to face three years of silence, three years of desperation and frustration.

I walked into the school. All of a sudden, I heard a loud bell, and everyone started walking fast, all of them spreading to different places without any direction. I stood there in the middle not knowing where to go. I looked around. No one was there except a big man holding a stick and moving it as if he were directing people somewhere. He turned to me and said something. I could not understand what he meant, nor could I ask. He repeated some words one more time but this time he sounded upset. My legs were frozen. My heart was calm but my blood felt hot. He screamed at this point, saying, "go, go, go." This I understood and I walked away but I did not know where to go. I did not know what was happening. I had a paper in front of me that had some numbers and the names of the classes but I had no idea where to go. In about three minutes, the whole patio was empty. There was no one around, only that big man and me walking away from him.

I tried to walk as fast as I could and I found myself lost. Lost in the middle of rooms that were closed and I had no voice to ask where to go. Far away, I saw a young boy and I decided to go to him and ask him for help. His response was "no español." I continued walking and there was another big man in the middle of the corridors holding another stick. He talked to me but I did not understand. He pointed to me with the stick to walk away. I walked away. He followed me. He continued pointing until he opened a door of an office and I sat down.

I was confused. I came to school but I was sitting at an office for quite a while. In my town you only went to the office if you were in trouble. I saw people coming in and out. I was there, waiting, but for what? Or for whom? I had no idea. Everyone was talking but I didn't understand one word.

About 30 minutes later an old lady came up to me and for the first time I understood someone. She said, "Que haces aqui." "No se alguien me trajo." "Dejame ver tus classes" (What are you doing here? I don't know, someone brought me here. Let me see your classes). She called a boy and he took me to a big room that looked like a gym. On the way there, he explained to me with half Spanish and half English that this class was my home period. I did not understand but I knew I had to go there. I walked in. Everyone looked weird to me. They looked different from the people in my town. There were some black, white, and Asian people. They were sitting down on the benches of the gym. The teacher talked to me but I did not understand. A boy from the back shouted, "Tu nombre." I said, "Mayra Nunez." The teacher wrote something on the paper and walked away. He did not smile like my old teachers and he did not say "welcome."

I went and sat down where the rest of the class was. Unsure of what was happening, I started to think about my days in Mexico; this is when I started comparing my life here and my life there. I started to compare everything. For many years, I continued this pattern, always remembering about my old town. Back at home, I was never confused. I would purposely confuse teachers. I was talkative and very self-determined. I was independent. I was Mayra Nunez Negrete, the grandchild of Manuel Negrete. Here, I was no one. I had to say my name every other second. Here, for many years I became someone who was not me. I was quiet. I was nervous. I was insecure. I was unsure of what to do. I had no voice, no opinion, and no ideas to share. I had many ideas but I was not able to share them. Comparing became a part of me. I was not able to talk so I decided to think.

After that class, I went to my next class but it took me a while to find it. When I found it, I had already missed 20 minutes of the class. The day continued just like that. I was late for every class, not because I wanted to be late, but because I did not know where to go. The teachers would ask me questions, but I did not know what to say.

Recess and lunch came and everyone was eating. I got in line to get my food but I could not eat because according to the people around me I was missing a little ticket. Unsure of what to do, I walked away and I went to a far corner of the school, close to my second period room. There I sat and for the first time I cried. I cried like I had never cried before. I was afraid. I was tired and hungry. I was nobody. This is where my pattern of crying began. For the next three years, this became my hiding place. I would go almost every day and cry. I would go and think about my past. I would go and pray to God to help me handle this time. I would always say to myself, "This should pass, too." It was a safe place; no one would go that way because it was the last classroom at the school and it was an ESL classroom, so it was not cool to be in that area. I enjoyed staying there. I would sing, cry, pray, and sometimes sleep.

The next two periods went by very slowly; people were talking and I was there but far away, blocking everyone around me. I could not talk and they would not talk to me. I was tired and nervous. This also became a pattern for me, always being nervous and unsure. When the last bell rang, I ran and ran as fast as I could until I saw my sister. For the first time during that day, I felt I could talk to someone, but I could not. My heart was beating, my tears falling, and she knew why. She had been through the same thing. She hugged me and she said, "Mija, no llores, estaras bien" (Baby, don't cry, you will be fine). My tears would not stop. "Vamos por una nieve." She said we would talk while having an ice cream, and we did. I talked to her forever that day, like I had saved my words just for her. I could not stop. I got home and did my homework and fell asleep crying. I was tired. This is when my pattern of sleeping during the afternoon appeared. Later, a doctor said I had a mild depression.

This was only the first day of school, but it summarizes my first three years in the United States. Every day, I compared; I cried; I stayed quiet; I felt insecure; I was no one; I was lonely. I would wait for my sister to pick me up and start talking. I would go home, do homework, and sleep. This became my life. I believe this affected my way of seeing life during those three years. I was very negative—always thinking about my past and not really enjoying what I had in front of me; yet I was able to pretend I was fine. Teachers never noticed that I was comparing the past to everything around me.

People thought I was mute, and I was. I could not talk. They thought I was rude, and I was because I could not respond to what they were saying. I had a feeling that speaking Spanish was not cool for many of my classmates; I did not want to make them feel bad, so I did not ask anything, not in Spanish, nor in English. I was quiet, always quiet. Always thinking.

Little by little and without noticing, my days became shorter. I found myself doing things that I did not do before. I was able to respond using a few words. My teachers in ESL talked to my sister and said that I was doing very well. My math teachers said the same thing. Here, I was an "A" student and again I compared this with my life in Mexico. I was an average student over there; here I became "Miss Intelligent." They did not know that I believed U.S. schools were very easy. I had already studied most of the things back at home. I had covered everything three or four years before. For me, school in the United States was a review. One thing I must say is that I felt really smart. When I arrived here, I was studying things that I studied in Mexico in sixth grade and now I was in tenth grade studying the same things. I believe this made me feel capable. I felt I could do it. Even though I would cry and I felt lonely, I felt very smart.

All my energy was concentrated on my school and grades. I became an honor student and I was able to graduate with a few medals. I was proud of myself. I believe that I was able to learn English because of my strong background in my first language. When I came to the United States, I had had 12 years of schooling at home and I was able to transfer a lot of things to my English learning. Spanish helped me understand a lot of things in English. I also had a very strong background in root words, prefixes, and suffixes that I learned in Mexico in my Latin language class, and this helped me understand English words. Some other things that I was able to transfer were capitalization, sounds, intonation, punctuation, and big words. For example, the rules for capitalization are very similar in Spanish and English. Sounds are also very similar— for example, the "t" and the "p," or the short "a" sounds and the "a" in Spanish. Intonation is very similar for both languages and also punctuation. It was really easy for me to transfer my knowledge to my new language.

I believe I did not struggle so much learning the language as I did to open up and speak, and I struggled the most with my inner problems. I felt lonely and lost; I had no direction and I was scared. My whole story is about my fears. I cried many tears. I suffered many things, but here I am sitting in my master's class telling my story. I am still struggling with my writing and my speaking as you can see. I've been here for 13 years and I am still not always sure if my sentences are correct or if my vocabulary is adequate. I try to read a lot to learn more vocabulary, but I feel that I am stuck. I feel that I learned what I had to learn to survive and I can't move beyond that. I will never be a native speaker. I have a lot of difficulty understanding text, my writing is really simple, but I am able to learn. I am a lover of learning, and that has opened doors to many possibilities. Also, this experience has helped me a lot with my students. I really take my time to talk to them and get to know them. I stop everything when a new student arrives, and I take my time to welcome and introduce him or her to the class. I find someone who can help the new child and I pair them up. I usually have a little box with crayons, markers, and erasers for them to help them feel welcome. I don't know if I am a success story but I know that I have come a long way and I will not stop pursuing my dreams—not now.

For the teachers of newcomers I have a few suggestions. I will start by telling you to take time to welcome your new students. Tell them that you appreciate having them there. When I arrived at my first class, not getting a smile from my teacher made me feel like an outsider. It made me believe I was not welcome. I felt like an intruder. I can't explain the feeling of insecurity I had because of his cold face. I still remember it and it still hurts. I was afraid and he made me feel even more insecure. Please take a moment and smile and say, "welcome."

Next, I would say to take a walk around the school and find that child who is crying or sleeping behind a building; take your time to get to know that child. I don't think anyone knows about this. You, my reader, are the first person to hear about my hiding and crying place. I went there for three years and not one person approached me and asked why I was there, why I was crying. Sometimes teachers would pass by me but they were in a hurry so they did not notice me. The funny thing is that the day that I was graduating, I was called to receive my scholarship and the teacher said, "There comes Ms. Smiling." Teachers saw me as a smiling student. They could not see what was going on inside of me.

Another thing you might want to do is find a friend or a nice child to help your new student. I used to dream about one child showing me the school. Every semester, I would dream that I had a friend, a friend who knew how to speak English and would translate and tell me why we were at the assembly or why we did not have school. A few times, I showed up at school but there was no school that day. I always wanted to know someone who spoke English. All of my friends spoke less English than I did. I was always afraid of doing the wrong thing because of my lack of understanding. One day, I sang my name because it said "sign" your name, but I read "sing" your name, and everyone laughed. My insecurity and self-esteem were lower than anyone could ever imagine. I want to tell teachers to try to help your students by pairing them up with students who speak the language, and please do not isolate them. They need to be around other children who speak the language. They should not be only with English learners.

Another thing, please take your time to get to know your students. They have a lot to share. They have history, they are someone. They belong to an important part of history in their hometowns. They come from places that you can't even imagine. They are part of a community. They are not aliens. I remember the first time I spoke in front of my class about my background. It was a summer class, during my junior year and my teacher wanted me to talk about my life in Mexico. I wrote an essay and I felt like someone cared. I felt full of energy. I felt like I had a reason to study. I wanted to be a teacher to get to know my students and their lives.

Last, I would tell you to embrace them with your love of learning. I would not be where I am today if it were not for Mr. Woods who always made me feel like I could do it. I met him during my first year at Marshall, and he always helped me. He was always telling us in Spanish that learning was the most powerful tool for anyone. I believed him. He would read to us. He would take care of us. He was an old, caring man. This was the only class that I walked into and felt like learning was taking place. This was the only class that made me feel that I was part of a community. He was teaching me English but he spoke "broken" Spanish, and I loved this class for that. He tried to be part of my culture. He tried to make me feel like an American. Please show them the power of learning by saying, "hola"; it makes a difference.

How Korean Helped Me Learn English

—Kylie Hwang

There I was, sitting in a seventh grade social studies class at Alexander Fleming Middle School. Mrs. M, a tall African American woman, spoke with a gentle, low-tone voice. Shaking my pencil nervously, I kept swallowing the dry saliva inside my mouth, which had been kept shut for hours. I looked around, hoping to find someone who was as lost as I was, someone with whom I could at least identify and empathize. No success. Everyone seemed to understand the teacher and the materials perfectly. They raised their hands and eloquently uttered sentences I could not understand.

What happened to my English that earned the envy of my classmates in Korea? Obviously, being able to confidently read "Good morning, Mr. Baker. How are you?" written in the seventh grade English book in Korea was not enough to help me survive in an American classroom. As I sank deeply in my troubled pondering, the bell rang. The rest of my first school day in America went the same way—I was lost, troubled, and dejected.

The key question was "How am I going to succeed in my classes when the English proficiency I needed, the very basic prerequisite, was yet missing?" Every afternoon, I would spend hours reviewing the class material and completing homework, which would take less than 15 minutes for other students. My English-Korean dictionary immediately became my best friend. Without it, I would have felt even more deserted and lost than I already was.

I knew that my first and foremost priority had to be acquiring English as soon as possible. After spending the first few days at school, I sat down to devise specific and tangible steps that would help me reach my goal of being a fluent English speaker. One of the first things I did was to take a portable tape recorder to school every day and record every lecture. When school was over, I always listened to the recorded voices of my teachers on the way back home. This way, I was able to focus on what was essential instead of unsuccessfully trying to write down everything the teachers said. At home, I tried to take additional notes and make vocabulary lists based on the recorded materials. I have to admit that it was tedious and cumbersome work. But at the time, I was determined to do anything that would help me master English.

As I began to utter correct expressions and understand what I heard, I started to befriend the kids in my neighborhood. I decided that unless I became more aggressive in making friends, I could not expect improvement in my English. The fact that no Koreans lived in the neighborhood forced me to use English even though I was not confident and still hesitant in my speaking. The neighborhood friends were accepting. They did not make fun of my mistakes or exclude me as an outsider. They were mostly my younger sister's age, but the three years of age gap did not bother me.

I now think that it could have been because I felt culturally and linguistically immature at the time. One of the girls, Crystal, taught my sister and me how to ride a bicycle with both hands off the handles. It was dangerous, but what mattered to me was that we were having fun. While playing with the neighborhood kids, I felt more and more at ease. I was able to be myself and say whatever I wanted to say, without worrying about making mistakes. I was gaining confidence, as I found myself more naturally conversing with my non-Korean friends. In this sense, I believe that Krashen's[14] "Affective Filter Hypothesis" held true for me. Krashen's hypothesis suggests that a second language learner is directly influenced by his or her emotions created in the process of learning a new language. Negative emotions such as anxiety, nervousness, or embarrassment act as a filter that negatively affects the learner's language learning process. On the other hand, an environment that provides positive emotion such as encouragement, affirmation, and acceptance lowers the affective filter or the anxiety, thereby facilitating the learning process. I was exposed to a setting in which I felt no pressure and thus was free from any emotional burden and stress. Such a setting greatly facilitated my English learning and catalyzed it in a speedy manner.

Another aspect that enriched my language learning experience was the DEAR (Drop Everything and Read) time given in my homeroom. I do not exactly remember if that specific reading time was still called the DEAR time in middle school, but the important point was that such daily reading time was being enforced in my school. After browsing the books in the school library, I chose a book I wanted to read. In fact, I immediately recognized the title, *Little Women*. The book, which I had read in a Korean translated edition, used to be my all-time favorite that I had always enjoyed reading in Korea. Since I knew the content word for word, I was able to read and understand *Little Women* in English. The sense of accomplishment and joy was indescribable.

The experience became the starting point for borrowing books that I had already read in Korean. Hugh Lofting's *Dr. Dolittle*, Lucy Maud Montgomery's *Anne of Green Gables*, and Jean Webster's *Daddy Long Legs* were some of the selections I reread in my first year in America. Because I had detailed prior knowledge about the books, my comprehension was greatly enhanced. I was able to handle the vocabulary without having to constantly refer to the dictionary. I felt more confident in myself and became consumed with reading. I had to thank my parents who had always encouraged reading since I was little. Never had I imagined that reading in Korean was going to facilitate my acquisition of English in America. When I encounter students whose families have just immigrated to the States, I advise them to start reading the classics they had already read in their first languages.

Until I entered college, I had very few Korean friends. Perhaps such circumstance acted as a push factor for me to acquire English faster. Nevertheless, my home environment

---

[14] Krashen, S. (1982), *Principles and Practice in Second Language Acquisition*, New York: Pergamon.

was still rich with Korean-ness, including language, food, culture, and literature. Unlike many Korean American parents who kept their children from speaking Korean in order to "foster" English, my parents did not stop my sister and me from using Korean at home. I still read books written in Korean in my free time and chat with my sister in Korean. Because I had always enjoyed reading when I was in Korea, the teachers who taught me in Korea used to tell me that I had sophisticated writing and speaking styles. Thus, once I gained enough confidence to speak out in my classes, I was able to transfer my vocabulary or previous knowledge into English whenever I had to write a long composition or make comments in class. In the process, my English improved while my first language never suffered.

I strongly believe that my firm foundation in the first language set the basis for the second language acquisition. Jim Cummins's second language acquisition theory also supports my belief. In his article "Bilingual Children's Mother Tongue: Why Is It Important for Education?"[15] Cummins states, "Children who come to school with a solid foundation in their mother tongue develop stronger literacy abilities in the school language." Through his research and theories, Cummins professes the importance of the first language in the process of one's second language acquisition. He concludes that both the first and second languages "nurture each other when the educational environment permits children access to both languages." Based on this argument, I also see the importance of interactive nurturing of both languages at home and in school environments.

One of the common questions that recent immigrants ask me is, "Since when were you able to speak naturally and understand most of what you hear?" Unfortunately, I find the question unanswerable, since the change was not an overnight jump but a gradual transition. However, if I were to draw an average time line, I would say that after about four to five months, classroom materials and what the teacher said started to make much more sense. Depending on individuals, that point might come earlier or later. Once I reached that breakthrough point, I felt like my English was improving exponentially.

After three months in the basic-level ESL class, I was placed in the intermediate level ESL class. The other classes in content areas were sheltered classes. After another three months, I took a placement exam and was placed in the advanced ESL class. By that time, I was able to take mainstream classes in all the content areas. Although I went through each transition in a relatively short period, I was still not fully confident in verbal participation without repeated rehearsing in my head.

One interesting aspect related to language arose a few days ago, when I came across my old term paper I had written in the fourth year at UCLA. As a senior in college, I had no problem in my speaking, listening, reading, and writing and also felt confi-

---

[15] J. Cummins (2001), www.iteachilearn.com/cummins/

dent about my linguistic ability. Yet as I was reading the term paper a few years later, I felt myself blushing with embarrassment. I suspect that language is a realm that can constantly be polished with more sophistication over time.

The English language acquisition process and its scientific and social dynamics are the areas I am highly interested in and that I want to explore as a future teacher and a scholar. My experience tells me that it is a complex dynamic with multidimensions. As for me, my own motivation to learn and the supportive linguistic environment were the main factors that supported and triggered my English acquisition process.

My Miseducation in the ESL Ghetto

—SEAKSAN PINEDA

Countless immigrants have traveled to the United States with their families in search of a better life. Many of the families that come to the United States bring their children to learn English. As the children progress in school, many have a hard time understanding the rules of the English language. As time passes, some of the children do not succeed and end up dropping out of school. I will be telling a story about a boy who was born in the United States, and about his struggle in school learning how to write, read, and speak English.

Many parents who migrate from their home countries have a difficult time teaching their children how to write proper English. Most parents cannot teach English to their kids because they never had the time to learn English themselves. The boy in this story never learned how to write in English because his mother never had the time to learn or teach him. She worked long hours in the day and long hours at night. The child suffered in school and was placed in an ESL (English as a Second Language) program. The teachers explained to the child why he had been placed in the ESL program. According to the school, the ESL program was an opportunity to improve his reading and writing skills and to reach the expected level of English to attend American schools. The boy understood why he was placed in an ESL program since he was aware that his English skills were very poor compared to those of the other students. However, he could not then understand why the school was teaching in Spanish. Most of the work that he was given was in Spanish and had no relation to English learning skills. As he continued to attend the ESL program, the boy learned more and more how to express himself in Spanish, and how to relate and differentiate the words and sounds of Spanish to those of the English language. But that still was not enough for the boy to progress academically in school.

Some of the problems were that the school allowed the children to pass without even learning the materials for that grade level. This happened several years ago when schools were allowed to pass students to the next level because of overcrowding. The school allowed the child in this story to pass because as new students arrived, the classes were getting too full and he had to keep on moving according to his age level. However, he never really learned according to what his level should have been. This was the situation not only for him but also for many other ESL children like him. Their mothers were happy thinking that their children were progressing in school, something that most immigrant parents had not been able to achieve. But little did they know that their children were not learning. When the boy arrived in the fifth grade, he was placed in a regular English class. He struggled with reading at the expected level; the child needed to read, but his previous classes had not prepared him for fifth grade reading. Yet, he passed once again. The child was afraid to ask his friends or teachers for help because he thought he might be humiliated in front of everyone. With this fear, the child taught himself how to read and write in English. He got books from the school's reading room or the public library that were simple to understand and were basic second- and third-grade reading and writing English skills. The boy was ashamed of his problem and hid his secret and never told anyone. Of course, this learning method was not the best and he continued to deepen the gaps in his education. The little English that he learned was not enough, but the child moved to the next level with a little more knowledge than when he arrived.

Learning a new language is very challenging and there are many steps that students must follow in order to be able to master the linguistic skills and to advance academically. Additionally, speaking the language is different from reading or writing. Speaking the English language was not difficult for the child of this story. He had television, friends, and other sources that exposed him to the everyday spoken language. Following the rules of writing and reading was the most difficult aspect for the boy to grasp because no one taught him about the rules of grammar.

That boy was me, never fully learned how to write, read, or speak proper English; I struggled in school and never had the chance to learn like the other children who were English speakers. To make matters worse, I was always being passed, but never being told what my mistakes were or how to correct them. According to the teachers, it was always okay—I would learn eventually. Now I am an adult and I am still struggling in college but I understand now that I have to work harder and that it is not going to be easy. To those kids who resemble the child in this story, I would recommend seeking help early: talk to your friends, family, and teachers; let them know that you need help and that you want to learn. I realize that I still have much to learn, but I will continue on, fighting until I reach my academic goals.

A U.S. Born ELL Story

—Amy Chu

I was born in San Francisco in 1987 and grew up as a second-generation Chinese American. My parents emigrated from Vietnam to America in 1979 knowing very little English. With their lack of English, they spoke Cantonese most of the time. I grew up learning and speaking Cantonese. Throughout my early childhood, it was all I understood.

I grew up living in San Francisco until I was about four years old. When I was three years old, my little brother Allan was born and my two sisters, Nancy who was five years old and Annie who was four years old, were already attending a preschool. Even though my two sisters were attending school and starting to learn this new language (English), it was never spoken in my home because no one could comprehend it except my two sisters. The ABC song was constantly sung around my home but no one ever spoke a real English sentence.

Kindergarten came too soon for me and spooked me. My mother woke me up one day, dressed me, and got me ready for school. "School—what is this place?" I apprehensively asked myself. We arrived at Jefferson Elementary School where my mother had dropped off my two sisters in a room behind a blue door. We walked across the small campus and came across these two large orange doors. My little brother who was now one year old was strapped to the left side of my mother with a baby hammock and I was on the right of my mother holding her hand. We entered the two giant orange doors and saw many parents with a bunch of little kids roughly the same age as me running around. I was terrified. I hid behind my mother as she approached the teacher and gave my hand to the teacher. "Who is this person?" I saw my mother walk away and then realized she was leaving. I started to cry, releasing myself from the teacher and running back to my mother. My mother stayed with me for a while until I was able to settle down.

The teacher had gathered all the kids to sit in a colorful carpeted area. I was still in tears and the teacher came up to me and handed me a giant stick with a big red, white, and blue cloth attached to it. She spoke to me in a nice soothing voice and I felt at ease. I held onto the stick with the giant cloth and she softly took my hand and walked to the carpeted area and sat in front of the kids and carried me onto her lap. The teacher and kids started to recite the pledge of allegiance, which at that time sounded like babbles in some mysterious language to me. I didn't know that not understanding a single word in English—since both my mom and dad spoke Cantonese only—would instill such fear and low self-esteem. I just wanted to hide when the teacher asked me what seemed to be like a question.

A few months later, my family had moved to Los Angeles and I was now attending a new kindergarten class at Griffin Elementary School. I had just started learning the basics of the English language; therefore, I was still uncomfortable with the language. When first grade came along, I was put in an ESL (English as a Second Language) class with Ms. Wong. Learning English in this class did not cause me any frustration or embarrassment due to the fact that every single person in the class was going through the same thing that I was going through. I was not afraid to make a mistake with the people around me. Most of the time, I spoke my primary language to my classmates unless I was forced by the teacher to speak English. If I had ever had a hard time pronouncing an English word or if I made a mistake, Ms. Wong would always kindly correct me. Second grade came along and I was put in the same classroom, with the same teacher and with the same students. I was familiar with everything.

Third grade was pretty much the same as first and second grade with the exception of a new classroom, new teacher, and new faces. I was still in an ESL class. The learning experience was not difficult. I had help all around. I made new friends who spoke my same primary language. However, after a month or two in that class, my family moved to a new community nearby. This meant an entirely new school, new surroundings, new teachers, and new faces.

I walked into a third grade classroom at El Sereno Elementary School that was already in session with a teacher named Mrs. Price. As I walked in with my mother beside me, every single one of those faces in the classroom turned and looked at me. The teacher kindly introduced me to the classroom, but what I realized was the majority of the students in the classroom did not look like me. I came to learn that their ethnic background was Latino/Hispanic. Not only was I struck with a new surrounding, with a new teacher, and new faces, but I was also struck with a new culture. I looked around the classroom to find anyone who might speak the same primary language I spoke. I discovered two people, a girl named Stephanie and a boy named David. I quickly became friends with Stephanie. Stephanie already had a best friend named Daisy, but she kindly welcomed me and we quickly became a trio.

In class, I had a hard time speaking up. I was afraid that my English was not as good as the English of these other people around me. I spoke Cantonese at my old school, even to my teacher because I knew she would understand me. But now, with a teacher who could only speak English to me, I knew I had to start speaking English a majority of the time. I started to practice my English with my new friends Stephanie and Daisy. Now and then, I spoke Cantonese to Stephanie, but I learned that Daisy felt left out when Stephanie and I spoke Cantonese. I forced myself to speak English more often, which in many ways also helped me learn to speak English more fluently. I was not afraid to make a mistake when speaking English to my friends, although I was still uncomfortable and frightened to speak up in class.

As school went on, I became more and more comfortable with the English language. Attending El Sereno Elementary School meant that the majority of the school population was Latino/Hispanics. During May 5, which is called Cinco De Mayo in Spanish,

I started to learn more and more about this culture. I not only learned about their culture but also had a sneak peek at their language. I was able to learn their Cinco De Mayo celebration song called, "De Colores." As of today, I am still learning something new about the English language as well as the Spanish language, whether it is a new word, a new grammatical rule, or something else. Looking back, I see that learning two languages at the same time—English and Spanish in my case—was one of the greatest ways to acquire a new language.

As I grew older and my English became more fluent, I was forced to become an interpreter. My parents came straight from Vietnam not knowing how to speak a word of English, trying to find that American dream. My brother had also started school and with many of my brother's parent-teacher conferences, I would have to accompany my parents to help translate. At Griffin Elementary my teachers all spoke Cantonese, so I had never had to translate for my parents. However, at El Sereno Elementary school, English was the main language and translation was needed for my parents.

Many times, phone calls from the bank or advertisements were passed to me because my parents could not understand a word they were hearing. House bills needed to be paid and because my parents could not understand the bills, again, they were transferred to me to write out the checks.

When my parents decided to apply for United States citizenship, I then became a teacher. I helped my parents learn the basics of English in the subjects they would be tested. For example, they needed to know the numbers, letters, and colors in the English language. They also needed to know about the nation such as the history of American flag, the presidents of the United States, the nation's holidays, and so on. As I was only 11 years old at this time, teaching my parents was quite difficult. During this time of my life, I did not understand how important it was for my parents to pass the citizenship test. I felt it was unfair for me because all I wanted to do was play with my friends and instead, I had to stay home and teach my parents. There were many times when I felt very frustrated when my parents were unable to pronounce a word or remember a date. I had to repeat it over and over and speak slowly so they would be able to hear the sounds of the words. However, after many months of practice and frustration, they learned the basic skills to pass the citizenship test.

Learning or teaching English takes a lot of patience. Many times, frustration and embarrassment is built inside when a person is unable to understand or pronounce a word. For teachers of K–12, it really helps a child when the teacher sits alongside the child and teaches him or her one on one. It relieves the embarrassment the child might have when dealing with speaking a new language in front of the entire class. Going at the child's pace of learning English also relieves frustration. To have time alone with the child helps the teacher learn the child's strengths and weaknesses and therefore the teacher can know which part to concentrate on to help the child excel.

Having a bilingual teacher assisting the child is highly recommended, even for an American-born (second-generation) child. Teachers should understand that even though children are born in America, they may speak a language other than English as the primary language; therefore, they may need special attention and assistance from the teachers. There may be times when the teacher may not speak the child's primary language. In this case, the teacher should help the student find another person that may better assist the child. In that way, the child would not be lost and he or she would have a greater chance of mastering the English language.

Overcoming My Insecurities about Learning English

—Alma Campos

The story begins with my grandparents who lived in a ranch in Michoacan, Mexico. As the years went by, they wished their living conditions would change. Although they worked hard each year, they were barely able to provide their family with enough to survive. They took the most challenging decision of their lives hoping it would change the future of their family. My grandparents decided it would be best if my grandmother came to the United States first, since she is an American citizen. She was born in San Francisco, California, and was raised in Michoacan, Mexico. My grandmother arrived in the United States on March 27, 1968. Soon after her arrival she applied for legal residency for my grandfather. While she waited, she worked cleaning houses and babysitting. After six months, she met my grandfather in Mexico City because they had an interview with immigration. At the interview, he was granted legal residency and was legally allowed to enter the United States. Although they both entered the country legally, their hearts were filled with sadness because they had to leave their nine children in Mexico. When they arrived in the United States, they quickly applied for their children's legal residency. Within two years, six of their children were granted legal residency because they were under age. While they celebrated the reunion with their youngest six children, they grieved for the remaining three who were not granted legal residency.

Once my grandparents left Mexico, my mother was one of the three siblings who stayed behind. My mother, being the eldest daughter and already married, was not eligible for legal residency. My family lived in a tiny adobe house in a small town in Michoacan, Mexico. The tiny house had only one bedroom for my parents, my two brothers, and myself. My mother was a housewife who had attended school only up to the third grade. My father, who was a farm worker all his life, never attended school because he was the oldest in his family and had to help my grandfather work in the farm. Both of my parents had little schooling and they worked very hard to provide for the family. Even though they worked as hard they did, it still was not enough to make ends meet. My parents realized that no matter how hard they worked, they would not realize the living conditions they had envisioned for their children. They wanted their children to have all the opportunities they had not had. My parents were determined they did not want their children to experience the living conditions they had known. They wanted their children to have the opportunity to go to school and obtain an education. They concluded that staying in Mexico would limit the opportunities and the possibilities of a better future for themselves and their children. They were encouraged by my grandparents to come to the United States.

My parents were determined to leave their country and begin a new life in the United States. The journey began during the summer of 1971, when my parents and I took a bus to Tijuana, Mexico. Both of my parents experienced great sadness when they had to leave my two brothers behind. My brothers stayed with my dad's parents. My parents felt nervous about the outcome of our journey. Three days into our journey, we arrived in Tijuana, Mexico, where we were fortunate to be able to make it across the U.S. border without having to show any legal documentation. My parents strongly believed that the crossing was less questionable to the crossing guards due to the new outfits we were wearing. I was in a brand new dress that my grandparents had sent to me.

Shortly after we arrived at my grandparents' house in Sun Valley, California, my dad immediately started to work doing construction with my grandfather. My mom stayed home and helped my grandmother with the housework until she later obtained a job at a factory. This was the first time our family had been separated but they knew this was a sacrifice that would be worthy in the end. Within four months, my parents were able to rent an apartment and save enough money to have my brothers join us.

My whole family was finally together again when my other grandparents from my dad's side brought my two brothers to Tijuana, Mexico, in a bus. When they arrived in Tijuana, they met my dad's cousin. He then successfully brought my brothers across the border to my grandmother's house in Sun Valley to reunite my family.

When my brothers arrived in the United States, they were four and seven years old. Within days after their arrival, they were enrolled in school. Soon afterward, I was exposed to the English language for the first time. I remember listening to my two brothers speaking English to each other and wondered what they were saying. By listening to my brothers, I learned some English words before I started school. My first school experience was when I started kindergarten. I was immersed in an English-only classroom. This was the first time I had experienced an environment that was very different from what I was accustomed to. The instruction in my classroom was all in English and my teacher did not speak any Spanish. I felt uncomfortable, insecure, and intimidated. I did not feel confident speaking English to the other students or to my teacher. My fear was that I would say something incorrectly and my classmates would laugh or make fun of me. During the school day, I remember being confused about things and having questions, but I was unable to translate my questions to English. Most of the time I waited until I got home and asked my brothers questions hoping they would able to help me. As a result of all the different emotions I was experiencing, I went into a silent stage. While in this stage, I just observed all of my surroundings. I would listen to everything and really avoided participating. I felt comfortable in this stage because it was what I considered my safe zone. Although I felt comfortable in this stage, I believe I was unnoticed by my teachers because of my lack of participation in my class. The following year in first grade, I experienced the same feelings.

During second grade, I was placed in an English as a Second Language (ESL) program that made significant changes in my life. My school implemented an ESL program for all second language learners. I was in the program for the following two years. Every morning, Mrs. Ellie Doud, a teacher assistant who was teaching the program, took me out of my class for about 30 to 40 minutes a day. Mrs. Doud would come in the morning into my classroom and take me and three other students to the school library. Mrs. Doud had a designated corner in the library for us to work in. I looked forward to going to school every day because I knew Mrs. Doud was going to be picking me up. Mrs. Doud taught me a variety of things: phonics, letter recognition, correct pronunciation, reading and vocabulary, and picture cards with related words. While in this program with Mrs. Doud, I learned the basic elements in order to succeed in the English language. Listening to her positive feedback and constant rewards reassured me that making mistakes was normal. I also felt that Mrs. Doud wanted me to be fluent and successful in English. Although Mrs. Doud did not speak Spanish, she took the time to show me that she actually cared about me. I truly believe that Mrs. Doud made a great impact in my life because she took the time to establish a relationship with me that none of my other teachers had taken. Mrs. Doud also helped me overcome my insecurities about learning a second language. Participating in the program changed my whole attitude about school. It helped me gain the confidence I needed to exit the silent stage. I was released from the program after participating for two years.

When I was growing up, my home and school environment were very different from one another. At home, I spoke Spanish to my parents because they always encouraged us to speak only Spanish at home. Their concern was that I would forget our native language. I believe this is the reason they never learned how to speak English. They would always tell me that it would be an embarrassment if someday I would not be able to communicate with some of our family members who spoke only Spanish. Because my parents did not speak English while I was growing up, I was also their translator. I would translate for them whenever we went to the store, when my dad had to give a job estimate, when they wanted to tell our apartment manager something, and, of course, when they went to parent-teacher conference. Being a translator at this young age was at times a bit stressful because I could not always think of the correct English words to translate what they wanted me to say. I believe my parents would notice that I felt unsure and then they would always say "no sabes" (you don't know). As years went by, I became more fluent in English and the stress decreased whenever I had to translate for them. After all these years, I still translate for my parents because they never learned how to speak English.

When I went to middle school, I was completely fluent in English. In high school, I remember passing my English classes without difficulty. Later, while attending Los Angeles Valley College, I enrolled in general English classes and other undergraduate courses. I remember having difficulty with writing classes. I believe it was due to the poor writing instruction from my previous teachers. In the past, I have always struggled with writing papers, but I have never thought it was because English was a second language. I do not believe that being a second language learner has caused me to have trouble in writing; but I do believe that I was not taught effective writing strategies. Having prior knowledge of writing strategies I believe would have made my writing experiences less stressful and frustrating. After completing all my general requirements, I transferred to California State University in Northridge, where I obtained a degree in Liberal Studies. I currently teach third grade in North Hollywood, California.

I believe that all English language learners would benefit from the following recommendation: students learning English as a Second Language should have the opportunity to participate in an ESL program for at least one hour daily. In this program, they would have their first exposure to English language academically and socially. During this hour, the students would learn all the basics of the English language; for example, the colors, the alphabet, the numbers, the body parts, and so on. The students would also have the opportunity to interact with other students socially. Placing the students in this type of environment would help them feel comfortable and less stressed when learning a second language. Another recommendation for these English language learners is targeted instruction for them. It is extremely important that teachers make modifications for all second language learners. These academic modifications should be done according to each of the students' needs. Once these modifications have been established, the students will have higher chances of being successful in the English Language.

Shying Away from Language

—Danthuy Vuong

Upon arriving to the United States at the age of 10, I was nervous yet excited at the same time. It was indeed a brand-new world with many diverse cultures living and interacting with one another under one roof. There were many things I did not know before, including the difference between Caucasian people and Latino people. To me, they were all Americans and I could not make a distinction between the two until later. My English was not well developed, although I knew a few phrases of greeting to get by and the names of the 12 months, ABCs, counting 1 to 10, the four seasons, and a few nursery rhymes. I was very hesitant to talk with English-speaking American people, as most new immigrants are during their initial stage of settlement. Despite my limited English skills, I was very inquisitive and full of curiosity to learn about this new land. However, what I did not realize at the time was that it would be quite a struggle for me to acquire the knowledge I wanted to have, and it was due to the serious challenge that I confronted in learning English.

During my 10 years living in my birth country, Vietnam, I was exposed to English every now and then through my father. He had acquired English skills by himself by learning through textbooks. Every morning he would sing to me a wake-up song called "Good Morning" to the point that I had practically memorized the lyrics. At that time in Vietnam, anyone who could speak English even just a little bit was deemed "special." I was taught counting the numbers 1 to 10 and the alphabet by memorizing a chart having a word next to the letter, such as "A for Apple, B for Boy, C for Car" and so forth. The only terms I could associate with the letters were those taught on that chart, which made my English vocabulary very limited. My father also taught me a few nursery rhymes such as "Mary Had a Little Lamb" and "This Old Man." He would sing those songs to me practically every morning and every night. My father was very motivated to acquire the English language, although it was hard to do because he could not afford an actual English teacher to teach him the proper pronunciation. As a result, his English was not only limited but with a heavy accent. Thus, learning English mainly from my father, I ended up speaking English with a Vietnamese accent. Greetings were the first conversational English I was taught how to speak. I learned the basic phrases of greeting and response, such as "How are you doing?" and "I am fine, thank you." And, to the question, "What is your name?" I would reply, "My name is Danthuy." These basics were the foundation of my English at the time.

When I arrived in the United States with my family, we resided with my sister who came here before me. Her English was very well developed by the time I arrived. She spoke both Vietnamese and English quite well, although you can hear a slight hint of accent in her English. She had two children: a two-year-old daughter, Cassie, and a four-year-old son, Tyson. Learning English was not easy for me at all. My sister is married to a Caucasian, and every time my brother-in-law would speak to me, I would always shy away and speak in a whisper. I felt rather intimidated even though I knew that he meant no harm and was very friendly. I was afraid to make a mistake and have people judge me, especially in this new land. In other words, I feared speaking to those whom I felt inferior to in terms of English proficiency. The only ones I felt comfortable talking to in acquiring my English language were Cassie and Tyson. Of course, their English skill was quite limited to a mere children's level; however, I was able to talk and use my English with them without feeling intimidated. I was able to learn the most basic conversational English from them as they slowly developed their language skills. I stayed with them for only a week, but I would come visit them every week for the next six years in which I was able to learn from them. You can pretty much say that the more they learned, the more I learned, in the same way that children learn a language as they grow up from base one. Most of the people around my sister's neighborhood were Caucasians. Every time I encountered them speaking to me, I used to shy away and become tremendously nervous. Whenever I would hear anyone who speaks loudly or speaks with an angry tone, I would easily cry. I was indeed very sensitive, especially when I had no idea what they were talking about.

In 1995, the year I arrived here in the United States, I entered Peter's Elementary School. I was placed into the fifth grade at the time and my teacher was Mrs. Hatch. I was placed in an English as a Second Language (ESL) class with other students. There were five students in my ESL class: four Mexican Americans and myself. A teacher assistant would sit with us and guide us through learning the English language. When I started to learn how to read, I would always pronounce certain pairings of letters in Vietnamese because the Vietnamese language uses an alphabet similar to the English one though their pronunciations are very different. In this way, although my pronunciation was not correct, it was easier for me to remember how to spell the words that I learned on spelling tests, on which I easily earned perfect scores. Whenever I was chosen to read a passage from a book, I would always turn as red as a tomato with blood rushing up to my head. I could feel my pulse rise to my temples and it felt as if they were about to burst. I sometimes pronounced the words in a Vietnamese accent, which sometimes made the class laugh. Although learning English in school was tough, it was better than speaking to people outside of the class. ESL classes did help me quite a bit due to their slow-paced learning, which is a good teaching method for English language learners.

When my family and I moved out after a week of residence from my sister's house and into our own place, I was able to learn the English language more easily. My new neighborhood had more Vietnamese, and that made me feel a whole lot better and more comfortable. I made six new Vietnamese American friends in my new neighborhood, all of whom were learning the English language as I was. I met a boy who was 11 years old and he spoke English constantly despite his horribly incorrect grammar and pronunciation. At that time, I had no idea how awful his grammar and pronunciations were. I just assumed that he was an excellent speaker. Soon, like this boy, I felt comfortable speaking English in my new neighborhood with the new friends I had acquired. Having more Vietnamese American friends (some attended my school) allowed me to practice my English without fear of being ridiculed. Pretty much, I was free to speak whatever I chose to speak without fear of being corrected or judged by those who knew the language perfectly well. I noticed that for an English language learner, it is better to learn through trial and error and to learn at your own pace rather than having a rigid timeline and strict corrective focus. I felt very comfortable speaking with people at my level and with a similar cultural background. I do not recall any bad experiences when dealing with teachers. In fact, they aided my language learning to a great extent by being very patient and cooperative. Nevertheless, speaking to native speakers from other cultures did not help me as much as speaking to people of similar cultures or a similar English proficiency level. I felt very intimidated to the point that I could cry if I was forced to speak more than I had to with native speakers.

In my experience, another source of acquiring English was through television, especially by watching comedy. At first, when I watched television shows such as Will Smith's "The Prince of Bel Air," I was never able to understand the humor. Though I could hear the audience laugh, I was never able to understand what was so funny. I watched and watched trying to understand the humor, forcing myself to laugh along when I heard the audience laugh, and listening closely to their words and practically squinting at the television. Finally, the day came. I finally understood the humor as well as what they were talking about. I was amazed; I did not know how or when I was able to understand, but I just did. I felt very successful and my face brightened like a child receiving her birthday gift. My English improved, but not to the point of perfection. I was still having trouble expressing what I wanted and meant in the English language. Watching television was not enough.

When I would need something at school and I did not know how to say it in English, I would always use gestures to express what I wanted. I would always insert some English here and there, but never in complete sentences. I could remember the time when I needed to get my lunch ID card to get my lunch, and I did not know how to say "ID card" at the time, so I drew a rectangle in the air with my fingers and said "square" repeatedly to the teacher. Of course, I was unsuccessful in my attempt to get my lunch ID card; the teacher had no idea what I was saying or wanted. School assignments were tough for me, especially writing assignments such as journal entries about a book you have read or a vacation you had taken recently. I would always become flustered when I received those assignments because it could literally take me a year to finish. Luckily, I had my sister's help at the time to write my journals, which helped me very much. I received perfect scores on my journals and I was really excited. Although I did not write them all by myself, I was still happy to see a good grade on the writing assignment. I read the journals over and over because at that time, those journals seemed perfect to me since they brought me good grades. I would read each journal entry again and again to learn more about sentence structure and vocabulary as well as grammar. Amazingly, it really helped me speak and write better when I repeatedly read my journals that my sister helped me write. Through this repeated reading and writing exercise, my English skills increased dramatically.

Looking back, my biggest obstacle in learning English was my emotional insecurity. I was nervous and fearful speaking to people who, I thought, might judge me just because I could not speak fluent English. That is why I became easily intimidated by the people who could speak English fluently. Accordingly, I was overly anxious not to make mistakes because whenever I made mistakes, I felt that people were laughing at me. In short, the lack of confidence and the low self-esteem in relation to my real and perceived lack of English proficiency were the biggest internal obstacles that prevented me from actively engaging in learning the language.

Reflecting on my language learning experience, I believe that the key to bilingual education is to provide English language learners with an emotionally secure and comfortable learning environment. Acquiring a new language is not an easy task to undertake, especially when the student does not feel safe and secure in his or her surroundings. As Krashen[16] argues in his affective filter hypothesis, psychological factors such as high anxiety, low motivation, and lack of self-confidence affect language acquisition of new language learners. My language learning experience provides an exemplary case for Krashen's claim that high affective filters have a negative impact on the ability of language learners to actively seek and use available language inputs to acquire the new language. English language learners learn best when schools and teachers provide safe and caring environments where students can freely express themselves without feeling fearful and intimidated. In line with this thought, I recommend that teachers should be more patient with English language learners by allowing them sufficient time and emotional room to gradually develop language proficiency through trial and error, without too much pressure and intimidation. Everyone learns at his or her own pace; no one (especially new immigrants) can acquire a language overnight.

In addition, teachers also need to recognize that English language learners may require individual attention. Not all students are born in the United States; in fact, many students are immigrants from various cultural backgrounds. For example, in my culture, we would quietly raise our hands to answer a question posed by the teacher, whereas students here would raise their hands aggressively shouting "Me! Me! Me!" This cultural difference makes it hard for students like me to adjust to informalities. It is rather typical for immigrants who are learning a new language in school to shy away and not to be as aggressive as the mainstream students. Therefore, it is essential for teachers to have patience and sensitivity toward each student in the classroom, especially toward English language learners.

---

[16] Krashen, S. (1981), *Second Language Acquisition and Second Language Learning*, New York: Pergamon.

Immersing Myself in English

—CARLOS GALDÁMEZ

*"The greatest danger for most of us is not that our aim is too high
and we miss it, but that it is too low and we reach it."*
~ Michelangelo

I still can remember every single detail of September 1, 2004, the day I moved to the United States. I woke up early in the morning and I took a shower. I walked around the house just to check if I was not leaving anything important, and as I walked I could not help but to think of how I was about to leave 15 years of my life and memories in that house. I remember talking to my sister about my future plans and how one day I was to return as a successful man; however, we both knew how sad we were because we have always shared a special bond. I was on my way to the airport by 4:00 p.m. because my flight was departing at 7:00 p.m. It was really hard for me to step out of the door of the house where I grew into a young teenager, and yet harder to see my sister drowning in her tears as I stepped out of the door. My dad took me to the airport, and on our way he was giving me his advice and teachings on life in general. I was only 15 years old, and even though I was sad to leave my friends and close family, the idea of being present at the time of my niece's birth in the United States made me feel happy. One of the aspects that made this trip special is the fact that this was the first time I was going to take an airplane trip by myself.

At the airport waiting room, I called my friends and my sister for the last time. It was a really crucial moment because I thought of not getting on the plane and staying there in my native country, El Salvador. I guess I was finding it really hard to move away from all the things and customs I used to have. I also was sad because somehow I knew that my grandmother, who at the time had suffered a stroke, was going to die soon. In the plane, I started to think about the number of people who died each year trying to reach the States and how lucky I was to just take a plane, present my passport to Customs, and be free to move into the States. Since my childhood I have always visited my relatives in the United States for Christmas, but this time I could feel that flying was different perhaps because the purpose of my trip was different this time. This time I was coming to stay and not just visit.

Within a month of arriving I started to attend Franklin High School and, like many young immigrants, I was placed in the school's ESL program. Even though the school was about two blocks from the house, the first day of school it seemed very far away. Basically, I spent it taking my English placement test and by the end of the school day they sent me to class; however, I did not show up for my last period class because I was overwhelmed by the school environment in America. I was not used to going to school not in a school uniform, walking to class, and seeing people with bright hair color; moreover, I was shocked not to able to understand most of the things they talked about. I felt like I was on a different planet, even though the students seemed to be of my own age. I could tell that we did not share the same thoughts about certain issues. For example, at the time I was scared of the group of students who were wearing only black clothes and had dark hair.

I was placed in ESL level 3, and I was happy because when they assigned me to that class they explained to me that my English knowledge was above average and that within a year I was supposed to be part of the "regular" school system. It made me feel better to see that other students, some of them from my native country, were going through the same situation. I remember meeting one of my first and to this day, best friends: Nattacha. She was from Thailand and had just moved to the states a couple of days before I did. The fact that she had a completely different cultural background intrigued me a lot. She was in my ESL class as well, and it was because of her that I think I was able to pass ESL 3 and then ESL 4. Nattacha was vital to my learning process in the ESL program because in order to communicate with her I had to force myself to speak English. Aware of the mutual benefit, we consistently worked together and helped each other with homework. She was able to help me with some of the aspects of grammar I did not understand and she would also encourage me to read books so I could increase my vocabulary.

I knew I had to make new friends and I knew there were two options: the first one was to just hang out with my other ESL classmates who spoke Spanish, or the second one was to make friends with those who did not speak Spanish at all. I opted for the second one and to this day I do not regret that decision. I knew the fast way to improve my English was to stop feeling ashamed and afraid of expressing my thoughts in English. Having non-Spanish-speaking friends facilitated this process. However, I hated to see how some of my ESL classmates interpreted my hanging out with people who were born in the states as a denial of the fact that I was an immigrant. They would ask me why I was trying to act like a "gringo," which I believe was their way of telling me that I was trying to "Americanize" my life. They would make fun of me because they would see how sometimes it was hard for me to explain what was going through my mind to my new friends.

As I started my junior year everything was different because I had completed the ESL program. For the first time, I actually felt that I was part of the school, and I also was proud of what I was able to achieve in a year. The idea of being on a different planet began to disappear when I started to understand the conversations around me and also the reasons some of my classmates behaved in certain ways. Because of the high grades I earned in my ESL classes my counselor decided to enroll me in Honors English. I believe that this class helped tremendously to improve my limited vocabulary and also to correct some of the grammar issues I had at the time. The teacher of the class, Mrs. Arrieta, helped me a lot and had a lot patience every time I had a question regarding the assignments.

Every day I was making new friends and I was meeting all kinds of people, yet I always tried to keep my circle of friends Spanish-free. Some people kept thinking that I did it to try to "hide" my roots, because once I was out of the ESL Program I stopped hanging out with the people still in the program. In contrast to their belief, I never felt I was drifting away from my culture. In fact, I was integrating American culture into my own life. If anything, I would never try to hide my roots because I am proud of being Salvadorian. During my junior year, I decided to take academic preparation (AP) Spanish classes to prove to myself and others that I was proud of my heritage and the beautiful language I speak. I obtained the maximum grade possible on the test. My junior year was good; but my senior year was the best school year I ever had in the states or in my native land.

By my senior year, I was part of the Student Body Association at school, and because of this, I was active in school activities and I was able to show the pride I had for my school. I felt attached to my school and I identified with the other members of the association. We all felt proud of our school and wanted to involve other students in our activities. I was also enrolled in academic preparation (AP) English literature class; however, I decided to drop the class, not because I did not like the idea of challenging myself but because I knew the teacher was not good. I was then part of the regular Senior English class with Mr. Martinez, to whom I owed all of my accomplishments in English during my last year in high school. There are no words to describe how thankful I am to him because he taught me how to take my thinking, writing, and reading skills to new levels. He would always encourage us not to believe what the media portrayed about certain issues; he would make us read a phrase over and over until we found the deeper meaning. Every time we were assigned a reading he would make us write all over the margins and to formulate questions about the article. In all of our essays, he would make a requirement the use of the Modern Language Association (MLA) format and he would emphasize the proper use of quotations.

During my senior year, I felt that my life could not get any better. I was popular and appreciated at school and there was a deep respect and mutual affection between my teachers and me. I have recently visited them to tell them how my college experience is so far. Some of my friends who are now seniors tell me that school is not the same without me, which brings a smile to my face, especially when I remember sitting there by myself at lunch during the first few days of school. There were some painful moments along the way when people would make fun of me and my accent. Yet, I had the last laugh when my name was announced more than three times for awards on graduation day and I was one of the first seniors to receive his diploma among the class due to my high GPA. Ironically, I was sitting on the stage and those who made fun of me were sitting with the crowd and below me.

I am now proud to attend California State University, Northridge, as a freshman. I have not declared a major yet because I still need to figure out what I want to do in life. I am currently working at the Hollister Company at the Glendale Galleria. Some may think that it is a place only for blond and stupid people. However, this is far from being true. I hate stereotypes and I love what I do especially because I get to meet great people and make friends and it keeps me active. I believe that my English skills now are good and at the college level; however, I know that there are many things that I still have to learn, to correct, and to improve, and I know that I will be able to achieve that over time. Spanish is present with me everywhere I go and with everything I do because there is no possible way for me to forget it. Spanish is way too beautiful. In my family we have a rule: Spanish at home, English outside. I use Spanish when I am with my family members and when I talk to my friends from El Salvador. I cannot imagine a day without listening to a Spanish song. I think English is an interesting language, but I am glad my native language is Spanish because I can express the same idea in so many different ways.

At this point of my life I think the hardest aspect of moving to the United States was my fear of not being able to be a part of this society. I believe I was scared that I would not be able to understand the people around me. Throughout these years, my family, my friends, and my teachers have made a difference in many aspects—my family for giving me the financial support to survive; my friends for understanding me and helping me to adapt to life in the United States and also for supporting my decision to apply to college and pursue higher education; last but not least, my teachers, for making me work hard to learn and improve my knowledge of English, for correcting me, and for encouraging me to become a better person and human being.

To those teachers and persons who work and are involved with immigrants, I recommend that they help immigrants to overcome the fear of speaking and learning English. I believe that is something that we immigrants have when we arrive in this country. We are scared of forgetting the persons and customs we had before by learning English, yet this will not be the case. To adapt to a new culture is a hard process; therefore, those teachers and persons working with immigrants should help them by showing them kindness and love. Encourage them to challenge themselves and to fight for their goals in life.

Section 3

LEARNING AMERICA
Acculturation and Identity Change

Introduction to the Section by Gina Masequesmay and Juana Mora

Acculturation

As our world becomes increasingly "smaller" due to rapid developments in technology, transportation, and mass media, societies and cultures that were once separated from each other no longer exist in isolation. Progressively, more and more people are moving around the world, carrying their culture with them, while adapting to new ones, and in the process, changing themselves and other cultures as well. To understand the changes that our societies and people are going through, various fields in the social sciences explain the patterns of changes[1] at several levels: the social (e.g., sociology on the transition from feudalism to capitalism), cultural (e.g., anthropology on cultural changes), and individual (e.g., psychology on changes in attitudes and self-identity). In this section we will focus on how the concept of *acculturation* is presented by various social sciences to understand how immigration into new cultures changes the individual and the immigrating group.

The concept of acculturation was first coined by anthropologists Redfield, Linton, and Herskovits in 1936 to describe cultural changes when two different cultures are in continuous firsthand contact with each other that result in either or both groups changing.[2] In 1954, the Social Science Research Council revised the concept to mean "culture change that is initiated by the conjunction of two or more autonomous cultural systems. Its dynamics can be seen as the selective adaptation of value systems, the processes of integration and differentiation, the generation of developmental sequences, and the operation of role determinants and personality factors."[3] In sociology, acculturation was linked with the concept of assimilation to discuss how immigrants can successfully adapt to American life by shedding their ethnicities to become Americans.[4] This notion of change at the sociocultural level has also been applied to the individual level by psychologists who discuss the issues in terms of acculturation strategies that immigrants employ to cope with the pressure of conformity that lead to shifts in values and behaviors. Since its conception, acculturation has gone through various definitions and operationalizations. Given the variegated conceptualizations of the term, we will discuss below how we wish to define and utilize this term.

---

[1] J. E. Trimble, "Introduction: Social Change and Acculturation," in *Acculturation: Advances in Theory, Measurement, and Applied Research*, edited by K. M. Chun, P. B. Organista, and G. Marin, 3–13 (Washington: American Psychological Association, 2003).

[2] R. Redfield, R. Linton, and M. Herskovits, "Memorandum for the Study of Acculturation," *American Anthropologist* 38 (1936): 149–152.

[3] Social Science Research Council, "Acculturation: An Exploratory Formulation," *American Anthropologist* 56 (1954): 973–1002.

[4] For examples, see R. E. Park, *Race and Culture* (Glencoe, NY: Free Press, 1950), and M. Gordon, *Assimilation in American Life* (London: Oxford University Press, 1964).

According to John W. Berry,[5] when Culture A is in continuous contact with Culture B, both cultures go through cultural changes. At the psychological level, individuals from immigrant cultures experience behavioral shifts and/or acculturative stress. Individuals who belong to the host culture also experience change, but not to the extent of immigrants. Depending on the context in which two cultures are in contact (colonial conquest, voluntary migration, political refugee, etc.), individuals from the incoming or invaded ethnocultural group have at least four different *options for acculturation* that are based on their level of desire for maintaining their own culture and their level of interest in forming new relationships with other groups.

Figure 1.1 presents a schematic view of Berry's conceptual approach to psychological and sociocultural acculturation. According to this figure, when the desire for cultural maintenance and interaction with others is high, the acculturation strategy is *integration*. When the desire to interact with others is high but the desire to maintain one's culture is low, the acculturation strategy is *assimilation*. When the desire to interact is low, but cultural maintenance is high, thus staying within one's own ethnic group and not socializing much with non-group members, then the result is *separation*. When neither desire is high, then we have a case of *marginalization* where the individuals do not fit in either culture. Corresponding to the ethnocultural groups' strategies are the larger society's strategies of *multiculturalism, melting pot* or WASP-conformity,[6] *segregation,* and *exclusion*, respectively. Applying this model to the U.S. case, we should note that the two cultures in contact are not of equal status. One is a dominant culture of the host society and the other is a subculture of an ethnic group in the United States whose members oscillate between WASP-conformity and multiculturalism. Given the high pressure to interact with and to conform to the dominant society, it would not be far-fetched to see that most individuals find integration or assimilation as their acculturation strategies. What is important to note here is that the acculturation process for an ethnic group and its members (i.e., an immigrant ethnic community) can involve strategies of assimilation, integration, separation, or marginalization. Individual members of immigrant groups may explore all of these options at different times in their lives and perhaps settle into one that best meets their needs.

---

[5] J. W. Berry, "Conceptual Approaches to Acculturation," in *Acculturation: Advances in Theory, Measurement, and Applied Research*, ed. K. M. Chun, P. B. Organista, and G. Marin, 17–37 (Washington, DC: American Psychological Association, 2003).

[6] The ideal of the melting pot is illustrated by the formula A + B + C = D (English + Greek + German = American). In American history, however, many groups who were not considered white, Anglo-Saxon, Protestant (WASP) found themselves in the midst of "Anglo-conformity" if they were to be accepted by "white Americans," a term that back then did not include Southern and Eastern Europeans and Irish Catholics, let alone people from Asia and Africa. Till this day, the notion of the melting pot is still a debated topic. Opponents claim that America has never been a melting pot where all cultures melt into one and there's no one dominant ethnic culture. Instead, they argue that there was a dominant WASP culture that did not change much and others added to the mix had to change. This is depicted by the formula A + B + C = A1.

Figure 1.1

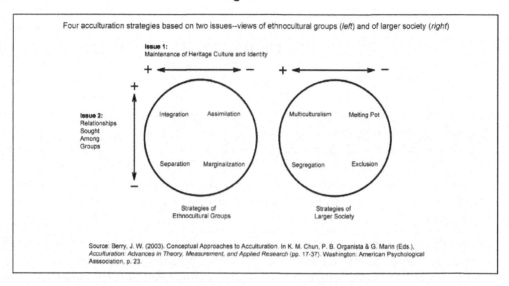

Four acculturation strategies based on two issues--views of ethnocultural groups (*left*) and of larger society (*right*)

Issue 1:
Maintenance of Heritage Culture and Identity

Issue 2:
Relationships
Sought
Among
Groups

Integration   Assimilation

Separation   Marginalization

Multiculturalism   Melting Pot

Segregation   Exclusion

Strategies of
Ethnocultural Groups

Strategies of
Larger Society

Source: Berry, J. W. (2003). Conceptual Approaches to Acculturation. In K. M. Chun, P. B. Organista & G. Marin (Eds.), *Acculturation: Advances in Theory, Measurement, and Applied Research* (pp. 17-37). Washington: American Psychological Asssociation, p. 23.

In the stories that are to follow in this section, the reader will find one individual using an integration strategy while another may utilize an assimilation strategy and yet another may become more marginalized when he or she cannot identify with either culture. The case of separation is seen less here given the high pressure to conform to the host society to survive (e.g., needing English to communicate). On the other hand, due to the increasing diversity in the United States and specifically, in Los Angeles, California, where ethnic enclaves exist, individuals can also grow up insular in their own ethnic culture or become bicultural by integrating both their ethnic and dominant cultures. In the case where there is no majority culture but many subcultures, individuals have more than two cultures from which to draw. In addition, the hybridity of pan-Asian ethnicity can be seen as an example of integration from American culture and a mix of Asian ethnic cultures. The complex nature of this identification process will be addressed in the next subsection on ethnic identity.

Ethnic Identity

Ethnic identity in ethnic minority children is not only crucial in social identity development but also serves as a self-protective strategy for coping with prejudice, discrimination, and stigmatization.[7] In this sense, a healthy ethnic identity development is crucial to the process of acculturation and self-identity formation.

---

[7] E. M. Vera and S. M. Quintana, "Ethnic Identity Development in Chicana/o Youth," in *The Handbook of Chicana/o Psychology and Mental Health,* ed. R. Velásquez, L. M. Arellano, and B. McNeill, 43–60 (Mahwah, NJ: Laurence Erlbaum, 2004).

According to Jean S. Phinney, *ethnic identity* is a multidimensional construct that refers to one's identity or sense of self as a member of an ethnic group.[8] In Phinney's conceptualization, an *ethnic group* is a subgroup within a larger context that claims a common ancestry and shares one or more of the following elements: culture, phenotype, religion, language, kinship, or place of origin.[9] Ethnic identity is, thus, not a static categorization but a fluid and dynamic understanding of one's self and one's ethnic background in sociocultural, familial, occupational, and peer contexts. That is, these contexts contribute to how one is to self-categorize ethnically. For example, if my family migrated here for a better life and from a desire to become Americans, then my family and surroundings would most likely encourage my identification as American. However, if my family and I left my country because of war, we might feel that our ethnic heritage is threatened by the pressure of Americanization and we might hold more dearly to our ethnic heritage despite being lectured otherwise by our peers and teachers.

In many of the stories in this collection, a common theme of wanting acceptance resonated for many of our authors when they were younger. In a school context that might stress WASP-conformity, assimilation was demanded of these individuals. Yet, because their phenotypes were not typically Caucasian, their acceptance as "American" was not fully realized despite their behavioral changes such as speaking English flawlessly. In some cases, individuals might feel that they belong to neither culture, especially if they did not receive reinforcement from home and peers to accept and be proud of their ethnic cultural heritage. In contrast, in a more multicultural context, individuals might find themselves being able to integrate being ethnic and "American" at the same time, especially if they live in a place where their ethnic community is well represented and thus are able to celebrate their cultural heritage and practice their customs. For individuals who did not face cultural conflict, a healthy ethnic identity development also contributed to a general sense of well-being and self-esteem that further enhanced their identity development.

Transnational and Hybrid Identities

When these concepts of acculturation and ethnic identity were coined to help us better understand race and ethnic relations in the United States, they were constructed with a simple and linear assumption of a host society or receiving country and a sending country. The belief was that individuals who immigrate to a new, host country adopt the values, language, and behaviors of the host country, never to return to the country and culture of origin. While acculturation and ethnic identity concepts

---

[8] J. S. Phinney, "Ethnic Identity and Acculturation," in *Acculturation: Advances in Theory, Measurement, and Applied Research*, edited by K. M. Chun, P. B. Organista, and G. Marin, 63–81 (Washington: American Psychological Association, 2003).

[9] Ibid., 63.

are still helpful in understanding the individual and group processes of transformation, the new reality of globalization has added complexity to these old notions and we now see new patterns of adaptation that are "transnational" in nature and a merging of several cultures into "hybrid" and multiple identities. In these stories, you will read about multiple generations of immigrants moving back and forth between two nations and cultures. You will read about individuals who live, work, and adapt to the new culture but also regularly visit the country of origin and maintain ties with family and friends. Latinos and Asians in the United States are changing the cultural politics of identity, using their native language and customs in the United States, influencing popular culture with their music, dance, and food and at times adapting new forms of language that include the rapid switching from one of the languages to the other as a new way of speaking and being in America.[10] In doing this, they are redefining what it means to be an "American" in today's multicultural, global world. Similarly, studies have also shown how transnational Asians (e.g., parents from Korea who migrated to Peru then to the United States where their children were born and who grew up to do international business in Korea, the United States, and Peru) have helped to recast the notion of ethnic, cultural, and national identity. For these transnational individuals who grew up and live in multiple nations and cultures where some still stress homogeneity of one cultural and national identity, the short-sighted vision of such assimilative pressures is thwarting the dynamic and creative reality of our new hybrid, global citizens. As teachers who are guiding the future generation, we need to be bolder in accepting and envisioning a multicultural and dynamic world and then to prepare our students to excel as global citizens.

---

[10] A.C. Zentella, *Latin @ Languages and Identities*, in *Latinos Remaking America*, edited by M.M. Suarez-Orozco, and M.M. Paez, 321–338 (Los Angeles: University of California Press, 2002).

Bibliography

Berry, J. W. "Conceptual Approaches to Acculturation." In *Acculturation: Advances in Theory, Measurement, and Applied Research*, edited by K. M. Chun, P. B. Organista, and Gerardo Marin, 3–13. Washington, DC: American Psychological Association, 2003.

Gordon, M. *Assimilation in American Life.* London: Oxford University Press, 1964.

Park, R. E. *Race and Culture.* Glencoe, NY: Free Press, 1950.

Phinney, J. S. "Ethnic Identity and Acculturation." In *Acculturation: Advances in Theory, Measurement, and Applied Research,* edited by K. M. Chun, P. B. Organista, and Gerardo Marin, 63–81. Washington, DC: American Psychological Association, 2003.

Redfield, R., Linton, R., and Herskovits, M. "Memorandum for the Study of Acculturation." *American Anthropologist* 38 (1936): 149–152.

Social Science Research Council. "Acculturation: An Exploratory Formulation." *American Anthropologist* 56 (1954): 973–1002.

Trimble, J. E. "Introduction: Social Change and Acculturation." In *Acculturation: Advances in Theory, Measurement, and Applied Research,* edited by K. M. Chun, P. B. Organista, and Gerardo Marin, 3–13. Washington, DC: American Psychological Association, 2003.

Vera, E. M., and Quintana, S. M. "Ethnic Identity Development in Chicana/o Youth." In *The Handbook of Chicana/o Psychology and Mental Health*, edited by R. Velásquez, L. M. Arellano, and B. McNeill, 43–60. Mahwah, NJ: Laurence Erlbaum, 2004.

Zentella, A.C. "Latin@Languages and Identities." in *Latinos Remaking America*, edited by M. M. Suarez-Orozco and M. M. Paez, 321–338 (Los Angeles: University of California Press, 2002).

Growing Up Poor and Asian

—ANGELA KIM

My family immigrated to the United States in 1979 from South Korea through an invitation from my uncle. They came for a number of reasons. The main reason was to provide a better life for my brother and my sister. I was born after my family immigrated. My parents wanted to provide us with a better education since English was considered a prestigious language in Korea. My parents thought that it would be a good opportunity for the children to receive their education in English. Another reason that my parents came to the United States was to keep my brother from being drafted into the Korean army. All young men in South Korea are subjected to the draft when they reach the age of 18. My mother did not want to take the risk of my brother being in the army in case of a war in Korea. The last reason my parents came to the United States was to pursue the "American Dream" that everyone dreams about. There were numerous stories in Korea about how wonderful and lavish life was in America. There were also stories that it was easier to get work and that living in America would provide a better life than the life that could be attained in Korea.

My parents came by airplane but they felt very uncomfortable leaving all the family behind. My father is the eldest son and he was the provider for his family, so he left Korea feeling uneasy knowing that no one would be left to take care of his parents and younger siblings. My parents were traveling to an unfamiliar land where they had only one reliable family member: my uncle on my mom's side. He was the first to arrive to the United States with his family and he was our sponsor. When my family reached the United States, my uncle helped my family to settle down. He helped us find a place to live and gave my father a job at my uncle's gas station. Because my uncle invited us to come to the United States, we came under visas but my father did not have a social security number and had to be paid in cash by my uncle.

The most difficult part of transitioning to the United States was the language barrier. Not only were the customs different but because my family members could not speak English and communicate with others, it became more and more difficult to live in this foreign place. One time, my father tried to get his license to be an architect because that was his profession in Korea; however, he failed because of the language barrier. My father would have to be fluent in English to study the vocabulary and take the test. Furthermore, my uncle was getting frustrated with us because we needed help so often. My parents were also frustrated because they could not take English classes due to their busy working schedules. My father was working all day and night at the gas station and he could only get about four hours of sleep each day. My mother was working at a sweatshop during the day and on some nights; she would take the night shift for someone else because we needed the money. My brother and my sister would take the local bus to school and back. My siblings would have to prepare their own meals and do their homework without help because my parents were not at home. Besides, my parents did not know the language so they could not have helped my brother and my sister with any of their homework. It was frustrating and stressful for everyone.

My brother and my sister were placed in an ESL class for most of their education. Although they picked up the language fast, it was not enough to be considered a fluent speaker. The title of being an ESL speaker was hard to shake off and the school demanded that both my sister and my brother take an ESL class year after year. They were not able to study with their peers and they made little progress. The ESL classes were not improving their English and soon school became tedious work for them. Doing the same work year after year and being treated as foreigners was not easy for my siblings. They felt hopeless and thought they could never succeed.

Throughout the years, my family went through many trials and hardship. My father started another job cleaning pools and my mother saved enough money to start her own wig store in Inglewood. My father had a very hard time keeping his customers due to his poor English skills. My mother always feared for her safety because the store was located in an area with a high crime rate. There was always a risk of her being in the center of violence because Asians were not welcomed in Inglewood. My family was robbed many times inside our home and in my parents' businesses.

I was born 12 years after my sister. My parents had to make a difficult decision when my mom became pregnant with me. Due to financial problems, my dad thought it might be better to not have me. My mom, on the other hand, wanted me despite all the problems and against everyone's opinions. However, after I was born, my mother could not take care of me because she had to keep on working to bring the necessary income to the household. Therefore, I had to be taken from house to house so that someone could babysit me. First, my paternal grandmother watched me for about three years; then, my grandmother on my mom's side took care of me for about two years. When I was almost five, I started to go to work with my mom because there was no one to be at home with me. My siblings were at school or work and my parents could not afford to hire anyone. When I was old enough to take the bus, my sister got married and my brother moved out of the house.

I had to stay home by myself since everyone was so busy. I had to wake myself up in the morning to get to school and come back home by myself after school. There was no one to help me with my homework and I felt abandoned, although my parents wanted the best for me. I was always comparing myself to my peers whose parents would drop them off in the morning and pick them up after school. I would have never thought that I would be in this position. Then, my parents decided to move to the San Fernando Valley because my sister had been attending college at CSUN and they knew it was a safer neighborhood. My parents had saved up enough money for the down payment on a house and my sister would help pay off the mortgage while attending school and working. Going to a predominantly white magnet school in the

San Fernando Valley, I felt that all my classmates looked down on me for things like having to take the bus home. They just simply could not understand hardship.

It was difficult for me to identify myself as either Korean or American while I was growing up. It embarrassed me that I was Korean since wherever I went my parents would always stand out as foreigners because of their "broken" English. It was particularly embarrassing at school when parent conferences took place. Schools in Los Angeles have Korean translators available for parent conferencing; but in the valley, it was different. I was the main translator and it was difficult for me to handle. If I identified myself as an American, the few Korean kids at my school would harass me and call me a traitor. They would classify me as "white washed," which meant that I had gone over to the white population and that I was trying to be part of the dominant race. I had a hard time growing up since I struggled with my identity, not wanting to be Korean but not being able to be American either. It was hard to grow up with all the financial problems and the hardship that my family had to live with. In my childish selfishness, I think I resented my parents for not being one of the middle-class privileged Koreans like the ones that resided in the San Fernando Valley.

Things changed again after my family moved back to Los Angeles, right in the middle of Koreatown, where I started to attend high school. I was scared because I did not know what to expect and the thought of starting all over was not too appealing. I would have to make new friends and I knew that the people in L.A. would not be the same as what I was accustomed to in the Valley. However, I was wrong in assuming all these negative thoughts. The school system was less demanding on me, which allowed me to pass my classes easily, and about 50% of the school's population was Korean American. The Korean students' economic status was similar to mine, which made it easier for me to approach my peers. I did not have to live up to this wealthy upbringing anymore. Because there were many Koreans at this high school, the teachers who taught my classes understood where I was coming from when I wrote my essays. When I attended school in the Valley, most of my teachers were white and they wanted me to live up to white students' standards. When I wrote essays, they were not satisfied and wanted me to conform to their ways in terms of both form and content. At my new high school, however, the teachers respected what I had to say and wanted me to feel proud about voicing my thoughts. I felt more comfortable identifying myself as Korean American and I found pride in who I am. I also identified with other Korean Americans who had suffered like me and my family and I learned that I just had to accept and move on with who I was. It was a hard time for all of us but my family managed to get through it.

Currently, my family is very stable. My parents managed to get their own market. They are now able to communicate with others in English and they picked up some Spanish along the way, too! My sister finished college and became an elementary school teacher and my brother is an engineer for the United States Army, which is ironic because my mother came to America so that he wouldn't have to enlist in the army. Both my siblings are married with children. I am finishing college this year and will become an elementary school teacher as well.

I believe that future teachers need to be more sensitive toward children who have immigrated from another country. I see many teachers inside my sister's school who are insensitive to parents who are not able to attend parent conferences due to their busy working schedule or to parents who are unable to speak English. It is a very difficult journey emotionally and physically to adapt to a new environment. Although my nephew is not an immigrant, I have noticed that he was discouraged from speaking his native tongue. His teacher wanted only English to be spoken and therefore my nephew has started to think that his native tongue is an inferior language to English. If an educator has such a powerful influence on a nonimmigrant, can you imagine how an immigrant child would feel? It is not that learning English should have a negative connotation but, as educators, we should also learn to value other languages and help children learn through their native tongue. I believe that as teachers, we can make a big difference in helping children feel a little bit more comfortable in their setting. The children are placed in an environment where they feel uneasy. They might not necessarily be comfortable with the transition. The children have to assimilate new customs, another language, and a different way of living. Peers are different and there is always that fear of being rejected. As teachers, we should try to make them feel included and that they are no different from their peers.

My De-Mexification

—Sandra R. Rivera Maya

"Wetback!" I quickly turned to look at my friend Mackenzie as she shouted in my ear and pointed to a dark-skinned man crossing the street. "I didn't mean you, Sandra, you are not one of them." A flood of thoughts rushed into my mind as I searched for words to say and all I could think of was, "I know I'm not." I truly believed that then. I stood by my words; at eight years old, I rejected my people, my identity, and everything my past stood for. I didn't want to be known as "one of them," a person who was beneath others. I resented my dark skin and black hair and wished so much to be lighter like my white friends with blue eyes and blonde hair. Growing up in a predominantly white neighborhood, I went to a local school where I so desperately wanted to feel accepted. I wanted everything my friends had—the latest fashions, hair styles, and latest music. These desired objects, which my immigrant parents did not understand, were my tickets to being accepted. My parents, who spoke English with a funny accent, would always speak to me in Spanish, and I would always respond to them in English. How I feared to hear them speak in front of my peers. It was so embarrassing; I could feel the stares and the giggles behind my parents' backs and mine.

Ironically, the very same thing I despised and rejected is a part of me. The culture that caused me embarrassment is the same one from which I came. Those people who didn't understand what was being said to them, their confused gaze, the blank expressions as they looked for familiarity in the English language—they are my parents, and I am part of them.

In kindergarten, I knew the many differences that separated me from the world around me. Spanish was my first language, the language of my ancestors, "mis antepasados," and I had to leave it behind with all that is sacred to a child: having a friend, feeling acknowledged, and being accepted. The feeling of isolation was strong and painful. I remember watching from afar how the other children laughed and played on the playground, but I was frozen in fear and hoped that one of them would approach me and invite me to play. I would often try to look at one of their faces to see if they would see me and smile, but when our eyes met, they would just look away. I stood alone during playtime and sat alone during lunch. I would wipe tears away as I heard and watched them whisper and point at me. Several times I would go hungry because Mary would take my lunch money while promising to play with me, but she never did. I would walk up to her and smile to remind her of what she had promised, but she would push me and tell me to "go away, brownie!" These images and feelings will forever be imprinted in my mind.

Once a day, I was pulled out of my class during math time and would meet Mrs. Ross in another classroom. I liked going there because she would talk to me and help me practice words in English and properly pronounce them. We did art projects, like ceramics and paintings, and sometimes we made snacks for each other. When it was time to go back to class, anxiety would begin setting in. Many times, I did not know or understand how to do a lesson and was afraid to ask for help because I didn't know how to ask. I remember often feeling very exhausted and putting my head down so I could feel a bit better, only for a little while. On many occasions my teacher, Mrs. Lanter, pointed to me and yelled, "Someone wake her up! Do we go to sleep in the classroom?!" I could hear the pounding of her footsteps as she approached me and pointed her finger in my face. "No sleep! Okay?! Bad!" I couldn't wait to run home into my mother's arms. I longed to be home. "Mami, porque no quieren ser mis amigos?" (Mommy, why don't they want to be my friends?) My mother would look at me with eyes of anguish and try to find a way to explain to her little girl why she was isolated and picked on. I remember she would often play with my long braided hair when she would have talks with me. She would tell me to just do well in school and practice my English. If I were to focus my mind on something, I would accomplish it. "Pronto encontraras muchos amigitos, veras." (Soon you will find many little friends, you'll see.) During those talks and consejos, she unknowingly triggered and reinforced the process of "my de-Mexification." I did work hard and practiced saying words and phrases in English until I no longer had an accent, or at least I could sound like my classmates. My looks also changed drastically, I cut off my long black braids and got highlights in my hair. I immersed my entire being into the American culture and in the process I lost my Mexican culture, the culture of "mis padres," my parents.

Immigrants from Mexico, like my parents, came to this country, like so many other people, for a better life. My mother arrived when she was 17 and necessity forced her to learn English quickly while attending public schools in the San Fernando Valley. She studied hard, worked late, and helped provide for her single mother and younger siblings. My father, at 19 years old, decided to leave his parents and six brothers and sisters in Mexico and travel to the United States in hope of providing for them by sending money from what ever work he could find. He crossed the border illegally several times, and several times he was caught by the border patrol. Never feeling defeated, he tried one more time and succeeded. He arrived in the home of a woman who often took in many distant travelers and gave them a place to eat and rest before helping them find their contacts in this foreign country. That woman was my grandmother, a person who has always helped and rescued those in need and one day rescued me from total assimilation.

One day, when I was 15, she sat me down and showed me a photo of a baby sitting on a burro. The image of La Virgen de Guadalupe was painted on the background. My grandmother told me of the many people who believe in La Virgen de Guadalupe and how she chose to appear as an indigenous woman to perform her miracles for the people. "She chose to look like you. Your beautiful caramel color represents all that our people cherish and hold dear. Your skin color represents our struggle to survive and our struggle to triumph over all adversities. The baby in that photo is you. And you represent me."

I traveled to Mexico years later with my grandmother. As we entered La Villa where La Virgen de Guadalupe is visually, spiritually, and emotionally present, I held my grandmother's hand and squeezed tight as tears ran down my face. I looked all around and all I could see were the same exact faces staring back at me. My people were here in Mexico and they were back home in the United States, all beautiful and full of humility and life. The longing I felt for so long, was gone. I was finally home.

My education has brought me far and has given me the opportunity to travel and meet many different people. As I become an educator, I bring with me a sense of humbleness and acceptance of other cultures and the knowledge to express the exquisiteness of my own.

English once was a barrier for me and now it has become my alliance. At first, learning English and speaking it without an accent was a method of survival for me in this country. Unfortunately, in that process of assimilating to American life to be accepted, I also learned to reject my Mexican culture and people, causing a separation between myself, my family members, and the Latino community. Being able to speak English helped me to communicate my emotions and thoughts and narrow the cultural gap. However, the culture that I so longingly wanted to be a part of saw me as different and therefore did not accept me fully. There was isolation from both cultures and a feeling of displacement and not belonging. It was not until I began to embrace my own culture along with the American culture that I felt completely at home, of being accepted and of accepting myself.

Without having a common language, many of us fall into a river of anxiety, frustration, confusion, and despair. Children need to be nurtured and guided through this difficult journey. As educators, our duty is to have children know they matter, deserve, and can achieve a proper education. Children cannot grow and develop properly if they are constantly being told they are different and that their culture or language is not important. English language learners need teachers who can give them patience and extra guidance in reaching the same goals as any other child as well as having the confidence that they are achievable. Through the experiences of my childhood, I hope future teachers will walk with these students who are most vulnerable and hold their hand as they transition into this strange land they long to call home.

Finding My Roots, Finding My Self

—Zenia Phomphakdy

Although I come from a family where both parents were born and raised in a third world country, where hard work and education are highly valued, my siblings and I were raised in the United States and didn't start to make education and hard work our personal goals until after a life-changing "vacation" that connected us back with our heritage.

My family is originally from Thailand and Laos. My stepfather's side of the family is from Laos. My mother's side of the family is from Thailand. Both sides of my family were in refugee camps in Nongkhai, Thailand, during the Vietnam War. They were in refugee camps because the so-called Vietnam War was also fought in Laos and Cambodia where communist forces were fighting against anti-communist forces that were backed by the United States. In the mountainous jungles of Laos and Cambodia, Hmongs and Miens were recruited by the CIA to fight against the communists. After the war when the communists took over, those who had allied with the United States had to flee for their lives. Many ended up in refugee camps in Thailand. Those not on either side of the conflict were also affected by the devastations of war and also had to migrate many times for safety, food, and shelter. The devastation affected not only the towns and villages of the countries at war but also bordering towns and villages in Thailand.

My stepfather's family had to move from their homes in Vientiane, Laos, and lived in refugee camps in Thailand. During this time, Laos was under communist control.[11] It was a depressing time for Laos because of dwindling job opportunities and poor agriculture. My stepfather's family was in a refugee camp for about eight months, and there, they began to plan their move to the United States. When the war ended, as refugees of the war, my stepfather's whole family was able to apply for asylum in another country. Leaving the refugee camp, they put their past behind them to begin a new life in the United States of America. My stepfather and one of his brothers stayed behind.

For my mother's side of the family who are from Thailand, they lived in Nongkhai, a small town north of Bangkok. The war affected most small towns like the one of my mother's family. Soon they couldn't afford to pay for food or other things to survive because my grandfather couldn't find any work. My great-grandparents were already too old to work, and my grandmother stayed home to tend to her 10 children. They lived in great poverty. My mother was the only person in her family who fled to a refugee camp. After the war ended in 1975, my mother was able to move back to Nongkhai. However, she did not want to stay in Nongkhai and was preparing paper-

---

[11] The Laotian people are still currently trying to overthrow the government.

work to file for her move to the United States in search of better opportunities. Some of my mother's brothers and sisters left Nongkhai to find work in the capital, Bangkok. My grandfather went to work in the farms as a vegetable picker.

In 1980, a Catholic organization helping refugees move to the United States granted my mother a loan and that aided her to leave her family for America. My mother moved to the United States when she was 23 years old without any relatives there; she had only a family friend who fled before her. My mother was able to survive because of the welfare system and began looking for a job. She worked as a seamstress. My older sister was born in 1980, a little after my mother's arrival. I was born in 1985. During these early years of difficulty, my parents separated, and since then, we do not know of my biological father's whereabouts. My mother has completed some college since she has been in the United States.

It was in 1978 that my stepfather and his brother came to the United States as refugees. Their other family members fled before them. His family also received a loan from a Catholic organization. With the help of the government, refugees like my father were on the welfare system and eventually were able to find jobs. He later became a U.S. citizen. Like my mother, my stepfather also attended college and earned an associate degree. Both of my parents are literate and fluent in English, Laotian, and Thai.

My mother met my stepfather in a nightclub through mutual friends in Stockton, California. They connected through their experiences from their homeland and the closeness in the Thai and Laotian cultures. They met when I was four years old and my sister was nine. They married in 1990 and my father took my sister and me in as his own daughters. A year later my brother was born.

My siblings and I were raised in northern California and were typical American teenagers. We never thought there was more to life than watching television, hanging out with friends, and following the newest trends. We had everything we needed and most things we wanted. Yet, we were constantly reminded by my mother, "You guys are very lucky." I now know why she instilled that message in us. It was because she wanted to give us a life that she and her family never had and to guide us to appreciate the things we do have.

The lesson that my mother had prepared for us was to send each of us to Thailand for about a month. At the age of 13 or 14, right before we entered high school, each of us was sent to Thailand to visit relatives. I was the only child who went by myself and this "vacation" contributed to the level of value I have for my life. My mother wanted each of us to learn about our ancestors, where they came from, how they had survived, and how they live now. It was the most transformative experience of my life.

I went to Thailand when I was only 13. My mother told me to take off the jewelry I had on. I didn't understand why until I walked into my grandmother's house. I remember being so excited to meet my grandmother for the first time, but I was not prepared to face the realities of a third world country. When I walked into my grandmother's house, I thought to myself how cute it was. It was just like those Thai movies my mom used to watch. Then I looked at the floor. The wooden floors had holes in them. From upstairs you could see downstairs through these holes. My heart dropped. I went downstairs and it had flooded from the rain. My heart sank again. The lifestyle is different. The smell is different. Everything is different. For the first time in my life, I learned to appreciate the little things that mattered the most: a roof over my head, a house that didn't flood, the convenience of indoor plumbing and central air conditioning. When I was visiting, it made me realize how people can live a happy, fulfilling life without fancy cars and expensive clothes, shoes, or houses. They value things that we, Americans, don't even think twice about.

Although I am able to speak my languages, my friends were not all Laotian or Thai. It was frowned upon that I was not literate in my own languages and that I was not involved in the local Buddhist temple. According to my family, these were all the things that made a Laotian and Thai person. If not, you were just an American who had forgotten about her roots and background.

Acculturating to American culture and my family culture required some juggling. I knew my family background, customs, traditions, and language, but it wasn't enough until I actually went to Thailand. Today I see myself as a strong Asian American. I have acculturated to the American culture because I was born in the United States. Simultaneously, I have a strong self-awareness of my Asian identity. I enjoy cooking native dishes and watching Thai-related programs. The one thing that I have not identified with is the native religion of Laos and Thailand. I am not a strong Buddhist follower, but I still strongly identify with the other customs, traditions, and overall culture.

Learning more about my ancestors and my heritage has made me value my family and the history behind them more. It makes me grateful for what I have and not to take anything for granted. I appreciate my life in the United States and understand what my family went through to immigrate to the United States. I now value the non-materialistic things in life.

When I went to Thailand, it matured me. The holes in my grandmother's wooden floor prepared me for the pot holes in my life that I was about to drive over. I honestly believe that my trip to Thailand influenced my mentality on life and helped me become a responsible daughter and descendant of the Laotian and Thai cultures. Fortunately for the family I have in Thailand, my mother has sent enough money for them to rebuild their home, and they now live comfortably.

Based on my experience, I recommend to teachers who teach students who are immigrants or refugees not to assume anything. Many people in general tend to offend immigrants unintentionally. This is a mistake that is often made. I suggest asking many questions and understanding the students so that the teachers can work with them.

I believe that Mr. Doherty and the other teachers in high school are directly responsible for me becoming a teacher. I also remember that mean fourth grade teacher at Magnolia. I always said to myself I would never treat my students the way she did. Some of my future plans are to return to college and pursue a master's degree in counseling and eventually dedicate some of my time to writing children's books.

As for my ability to speak English, I still find myself struggling with certain parts of it. I feel that my Spanish and my English are not at the level I wish they could be. I do enjoy reading in both English and Spanish. At one point in my life I wanted to get rid of my accent. However, during my college years I met a professor who made me realize that if I lost my accent it would be like losing a part of my identity and where I came from. I have an accent because I am an immigrant from El Salvador. That is part of my uniqueness and now I can claim to be proud of it!

Adventures in (Pan) Ethnicity

—Jean-Paul deGuzman

Initial Thoughts

American by birth; Filipino by blood; Asian American by choice. Yes, I have proudly marched in those seminal Filipino/Catholic *Flores de Mayo* festivals; I frequent the various stores that compose *Pinoy Avenue* on a weekly basis; my bookshelf is filled with titles such as *America Is in the Heart*, *Philippine Society and Revolution*, *Creating Masculinity in Los Angeles' Little Manila,* and, of course, the influential *Filipinos: The Forgotten Asian Americans*. I identify as Filipino American, but often I am quick to add Asian American to that description. Why this distinction? In this essay, I provide a snapshot of my journey through ethnic identity development. Going from an outlook—albeit not of my own choosing—of unexamined color blindness and assimilation, to feelings of disconnection and isolation, and finally the revelation of the inclusion, possible with panethnicity, I illustrate that there is more to ethnic identity than meets the eye.

Growing Up American

"Oh, are you Filipino?"

"No, I'm an American!"

This was my assertive response to an elderly European American woman who took pride in her apparent ability to discern my ethnic heritage. That exchange occurred when I was about eight or nine and encapsulates my initial configurations of identity. I should stress, however, that mine was hardly the "typical" childhood. Born to a single, first-generation immigrant mother from the Philippines, who worked at least two to three jobs when I was growing up, I was generally cared for by a loving and all-American, World War II veteran white woman. Indeed, while other second-generation Asian Americans probably reflect on the indignities of bringing ethnic foods with pungent smells to school for lunch (while all the "normal" kids had sandwiches) and thus not fitting in, I didn't have such concerns. I was reared on meat and potatoes—and a healthy dose of color blindness.

That loving surrogate grandmother—a woman who gained that position by simply being a generous neighbor who didn't mind looking after a small brown child—taught me that at the end of the day we're all Americans. Lurking behind that life lesson I now know was a less than subtle call for assimilation. But when you're in elementary school, fitting in, no matter what, was the supreme priority. In my elementary and middle school days, I was just one of a handful of Filipinos and indeed Asians in my schools. We never consciously hung out together in some sort of proto-activist statement about resistance and solidarity. Honestly, I do not remember any systematic attempts by white students to force me to the margins, to ostracize me, or to make me an "other" just because my skin happened to be a different color (or perhaps, my mind has jettisoned those less than savory memories). In any case, we all just insisted on being kids. Such a naïve view wouldn't last for long. As I journeyed through high school, various classmates—both white and Asian—asserted that at the end of the day we *weren't* all just Americans, and this got me thinking.

Off to High School

It was at my Catholic high school that my thoughts on ethnicity and identity crystallized. While I often took solace and pride in my citizenship in my high school community—pep rallies, club activities, dances, and the like—my participation in Filipino American communities was another, more fractured story. Racial categories were entrenched at the school. Composing some 60% of the school population, whites were, of course, at the top of every hierarchy conceivable. However, Filipino Americans (some 20% of the school) posed a certain challenge to the dominance of whites. Many of those Filipino Americans had gone to parochial elementary schools that were predominantly Filipino (and Latina/o). Their social networks were already well established long before they came to high school. When they came to high school, given their strength in numbers and their networks, they were able to challenge the racial logic that normalized whites as the most popular and students of color as subordinated. In other words, they had the benefit of coming to high school already with a sense of empowerment. So, when confronted with stereotypes or other negative feelings about Filipinos, they could rely on their networks and they developed an oppositional sense of pride. In other words, they were proud to be Filipino Americans in the face of the prejudices of white students.

Here is where my narrative enters. The ethnic division between groups was evident when I enrolled. I quickly learned that my childhood color-blind view toward the world was not applicable. I clearly did not fit in with the white students, so where did that leave me? Although I was tempted to feel empowered by the sheer number of Filipino Americans at the school and their embrace of a Filipino American identity, the distance from and tension with that community immediately became evident. Coming from a nonreligious middle school and not one of my high school's Catholic, predominantly Filipino American feeder elementary schools, I was estranged from their already well-established social network that extended far beyond the alabaster walls of our school. That rift, combined with my lack of desire to adopt various accoutrements of their burgeoning Filipino American cultural nationalism (e.g., styles of dress, music, transportation, and ethnolinguistics) meant I was a persona non grata in their eyes.

But of course, it is important to remember that a theme that resonates with youth across time and space is, again, fitting in. The cultural nationalists were cool, let's be honest. And to make them even more appealing, they were cool in a subversive manner. They had the best parties, the best-looking people, the fastest cars, and the best clothes. That they combined all of that with *pride* in being Filipino American made them all the more attractive.

The exclusion and ostracism stung, as anyone could imagine, but I tried hard not to pay them too much attention. Instead, I tried to find like-minded Asian American/ Filipino American friends, many of whom were not "those" types of Filipino Americans. (And, of course, I am cognizant of the fact that I was probably derided as one of "those" Filipino Americans who did not conform to arbitrary standards of "authenticity.") I left high school with an ambivalent feeling about my ethnic identity. Certain peers reminded me I was not a Filipino American. I didn't feel very American any more as whiteness defined normalcy and Filipino Americans contested that and created an alternative understanding of normalcy (one to which I was not privy). Being an Asian American at this moment in my life meant simply being an Asian person who was living in America, and not a Filipino American.

College and Consciousness

Flashing forward to my undergraduate years at a state university in suburban Los Angeles, I came to Asian American Studies (AAS) by accident. Officially a history major, I ventured into an introductory class in Asian American Studies armed with a slight desire to learn about that nebulous category of "Asian American," but with a more pressing desire to fulfill a general education requirement. Something, however, clicked and within a semester I became a full-fledged Asian American Studies major. Initially I was attracted to the relevant curriculum—totally new, fresh and (forgive the cliché) "cutting edge" courses—put forth in smaller, more supportive and intimate classes, generally infused with a social justice agenda. As was true of most AAS majors, my education was an eye-opener. My courses also precipitated a reevaluation of my high school experiences.

As my consciousness of social issues grew, I felt that I could return to my less than idyllic understandings of and experiences with the Filipino American communities that surrounded me. Shunned from the core group of Filipino Americans at my high school, I was confident that in the collegiate setting, I would avoid such myopia. I eagerly attended meetings of the resident Filipino American student organization, assuming I had arrived. However, I was mistaken. Despite my enthusiasm, I never really connected with anyone, nor did anyone really attempt to connect with me. Conversations with the few people I did know generally focused on their ensuring that I pay membership dues in a timely fashion. Because I did not dress a certain way, because I did not speak a certain way, because I did not have friends already well established in the organization—because of this, because of that, I was shunned. Not fitting the archetype of what a member of that group should be, I retreated to and helped build the Asian American Studies Student Association—in my opinion, a more progressive body that thrived on the ethnic, cultural, class, and linguistic diversity of its membership. If anything, the diverse composition of our organization helped us focus attention on an equally diverse sampling of issues that enabled and empowered our sense of being Asian Americans and People of Color in a racialized, unequal society.

My experiences here taught me that panethnicity is not just an amalgamation of diverse ethnicities blindly calling themselves "Asian American" or "Asian Pacific Islander." Rather, panethnicity is an identity and a *process* that at once involves a recognition of and respect for difference while also recognizing the similar ways that we Filipinos, Koreans, Thais, Cambodians, Vietnamese, Chinese, Japanese, and others have been treated and managed by the dominant society.

However, panethnicity incorporates and goes beyond identity conceptualization. It is a political project that requires action, education, and transformation. Given that Southeast Asian Americans are generally marginalized, even in Asian American Studies curricula, we organized a tour of the Thai American community in the San Fernando Valley. To address the rise in hate crimes against Middle Eastern Americans and South Asian Americans in the wake of September 11, 2001 (paralleling the anti-Japanese agitation following the bombing of Pearl Harbor), we organized a conference that brought together leaders of the local Muslim, South Asian, and Japanese American communities to speak to the university community. Significantly, at that time, no one in our organization actually identified as a Muslim, Middle Eastern, or South Asian. Our organizing signified that Asian American panethnicity is not circumscribed by any one ethnicity but was organized around solidarity. As these short examples highlight, to me, panethnicity is about the merger between ideas and action—in other words, praxis. Panethnicity is not easy, however. It requires a great dose of reflexivity to recognize and critique the differential privileges and biases we all had, based on our respective ethnicities, genders, and sexualities. It was indeed difficult coming to terms with that self-reflexivity, but in constant self-examination—for me at least—my panethnic identity became all the stronger.

Final Thoughts

This section is not intended to be a sweeping indictment of "the" Filipino American "community," as if *one* could ever really exist. Rather, I have provided a glimpse into what ethnicity has meant to me over the span of my relatively short life. On the one hand, it meant exclusion; on the other, it meant empowerment and change. From my experience, I can see how cultural nationalism has the potential to unify the subordinated of society and foster a sense of pride. Cultural nationalism can and indeed does empower many people. However, more often than not, I have been the recipient of the flip side. Those lessons in (in)authenticity have taught me the values of going beyond our respective ethnic group for self and social empowerment. The collective teachings over these years have imparted to me the value of a panethnic identity, one that is born of shared experiences and is exercised to effect change.

Also, I think that the experiences I outlined above are instructive for culturally sensitive teachers. In elementary school, I was taught to generally erase differences. This of course, did not equip me for the "real" world where multiple identities can both fragment and unify our lives. Therefore, a critical approach to multicultural education at the earliest stages might set students on a right path to understanding themselves and the world they live in. We do have differences; some of us look different than others. It is important for teachers to be "real" about this simple fact with their students, and to take it one step further to look at how those differences might be manifested in popularity—and down the road, power. Indeed, difference exists within groups. It is important that teachers avoid looking at one group and assuming it speaks for the whole for, as I have explained, belonging is not universal. In order for there to be a sense of inclusion, someone must be excluded.

So, the question remains, how do you teach against aggressive, uncritical cultural nationalism? A singular answer is elusive. Again, teachers—particularly those in social studies—need to go beyond basic multicultural curricula. While learning about the different heroes and holidays of various ethnic groups might be a start, teachers must uncover the dynamics of power in our society, to highlight how institutions oppress people and how those on the margins have fought back, particularly through coalition building. Then, the task is to get students thinking about how all of those practices are manifested in their lives. This approach might leave students with a vastly more textured comprehension of how their lives and identities intersect with larger historical and contemporary currents.

ABOUT OUR CO-EDITORS

Juana Mora

I was born in Jalisco, Mexico, and immigrated to the United States with my parents and seven siblings in 1960. I am the first member of my family to attend college. I worked after school to help my family and received financial support to attend the University of California at Santa Cruz where I completed my B.A. in linguistics. I later received a Ford Foundation Fellowship to attend Stanford University where I completed my Ph.D. in education in 1984. My early work was on Latina/o culturally focused substance abuse treatment and prevention and I have taught courses on Latino families, women, health, and education. My current work is on the development of community-based research partnerships for the improvement of Latino community health. In 2002, I co-edited a book titled *Latino Social Policy: A Participatory Research Model,* which highlights lessons learned and identifies best practices from Latino community studies designed and implemented in a participatory manner. I am currently a professor in the Chicana/o Studies Department at California State University, Northridge.

Gina Masequesmay

I was born in Saigon, Vietnam, and left the country for France when I was six years old. My family moved to France and then to the United States in late 1977. I grew up in the "Valley" and only moved out when I went to Pomona College in Claremont. I graduated in 1991 with a B.A. in sociology and decided to try out social work for two years. I returned to school, enrolling in a graduate program in sociology at UCLA. I earned my Ph.D. in 2001 and began teaching at California State University, Northridge (CSUN) three days after I filed my dissertation. My research interests are on immigrant adaptation, Vietnamese Americans, and the intersection of race, ethnicity, class, gender, and sexuality. I am now associate professor in Asian American Studies, where I served as interim chair in 2007. I am currently enjoying a sabbatical and will travel to Vietnam to explore new research on Vietnamese Buddhism, helping and healing, and negotiating transnational identities.

Ana Sánchez Muñoz

I was born in Spain. I graduated from the University of Salamanca with a B.A. in philology (major in English linguistics and literatures of the English-speaking countries with minors in French and Italian). I came to the United States in 2000 and I have been living in Los Angeles since then. I started my doctoral studies in 2001. I graduated from the University of Southern California in 2007 with a Ph.D. in Hispanic linguistics. My research interests include language variation and change, bilingualism, language acquisition, and situations of language contact. In particular, I am interested in situations of contact between Spanish and English in the United States and in studying how Spanish is developed, used, and maintained by heritage speakers of Spanish in the United States. Currently, I am an assistant professor in the Department of Chicana/o Studies at California State University, Northridge (CSUN), where I teach language acquisition and language development in Chicana/o and ESL speakers. I am also a faculty member of the linguistics program at CSUN.

Eunai Shrake

I was born in Korea and came to the United States as an international student for my graduate degree. I graduated from UCLA in 1996 with a Ph.D. in education with a concentration on social sciences and comparative education. I am currently an associate professor in the Department of Asian American Studies at California State University at Northridge where I teach courses on multicultural education with a special emphasis on Asian American students and their culture. My research focuses on cross-cultural studies in the areas of parenting styles, ethnic identity development, and adolescent problem behaviors.

RESOURCE BIBLIOGRAPHY

Asian American Curriculum Project. www.asianamericanbooks.com.

Applebaum, Peter Michael. *Multicultural and Diversity Education: A Reference Handbook*. Santa Barbara, CA: ABC-CLIO, 2002.

August, Diane and Kenji Hakuta. *Improving Schooling for Language-minority Children: A Research Agenda*. Washington, DC: National Academy Press, 1997.

Baker, Colin. *Foundations of Bilingual Education and Bilingualism*, 4th ed. Clevedon, UK: Multilingual Matters, 2006.

Banks, James A., ed. *Handbook of Research on Multicultural Education*. San Francisco: Jossey-Bass, 2004.

Callahan, Rebecca M. "Tracking and High School English Learners: Limiting Opportunity to Learn." *American Educational Research Journal* 42(2)(2005): 305–328.

Crawford, James. *Bilingual Education: History, Politics, Theory and Practice,* 2d ed. Los Angeles, CA: Bilingual Educational Services, 1991.

Crawford, James, ed. *At War with Diversity: U.S. Language Policy in an Age of Anxiety*. Clevedon, UK: Multilingual Matters, 2000.

Chan, Sucheng. *Asian Americans: An Interpretive History*. Boston: Twayne, 1991.

Darder, Antonia. *Culture and Power in the Classroom: A Critical Foundation for Bicultural Education*. New York: Bergin & Garvey, 1991.

Darder, Antonia, Rodolfo D. Torres, and Henry Gutierrez, eds. *Latinos and Education: A Critical Reader*. New York: Routledge, 1997.

De la Torre, William and Christina U. Ayala-Alcantar, eds. *Education in American Society*. Dubuque, IA: Kendall/Hunt, 2003.

Delgado-Gaitan, Concha and Henry Trueba. *Crossing Cultural Borders: Education for Families in America*. London: Falmer Press, 1991.

Delgado-Gaitan, Concha. *Literacy for Empowerment: The Role of Parents in Children's Education*. New York: Falmer Press, 1990.

Eggen, Paul D. and Donald P. Kauchak. *Educational Psychology: Windows on Classrooms*. 6th ed. Upper Saddle River, NJ: Prentice Hall, 2003.

Elkholy, John and Francine Hallcom, eds. *The Teacher' Guide to Culture and Linguistics*. Dubuque, IA: Kendall/Hunt, 2005.

Escuela. Videocassette. Produced by Border Pictures, Inc. Director Hannah Weyer. New York: Women Make Films, 2002.

Espinoza-Herold, Mariella. *Issues in Latin Education: Race, School Culture, and the Politics of Academic Success.* Boston: Allyn and Bacon, 2003.

Espiritu, Yen Le. *Asian American Panethnicity: Bridging Institutions and Identities.* Philadelphia: Temple University Press, 1992.

Faltis, Christian J. and Paula Wolfe, eds. *So Much to Say: Adolescents, Bilingualism, and ESL in the Secondary School.* New York: Teachers College Press, 1999.

Freire, Paulo. *Education for Critical Consciousness.* New York: Continuum, 1981.

Freire, Paulo. *Pedagogy of the Oppressed.* New York: Continuum, 1993.

Fry, Richard. *Latinos in Higher Education: Many Enroll, Too Few Graduate.* Pew Hispanic Center, 2002. http://pewhispanic.org/files/reports/11.pdf.

Fry, Richard. *Hispanic Youth Dropping Out of U.S. Schools: Measuring the Challenge.* 2003. http://pewhispanic.org/files/reports/19.pdf.

Fong, Timothy P. *The Contemporary Asian American Experience: Beyond the Model Minority.* Upper Saddle River, NJ: Prentice Hall, 1998.

Furumoto, Rosa Linda. *Mexicanas Valientes: Critical Consciousness among School Parent Leaders.* Diss. University of California, Los Angeles, 2001. Ann Arbor: UMI, 2002.

Hallcom, Francine. *A Guide to Linguistics for E.S.L. Teachers.* Dubuque, IA: Kendall/Hunt, 1995.

Harry, Beth. *Teacher's Handbook for Cultural Diversity, Families, and the Special Education System, Communication and Empowerment.* New York: Teachers College Press, 1997.

Hirabayashi, Lane Ryo, ed. *Teaching Asian America: Diversity and the Problem of Community.* Lanham, MD: Rowman & Littlefield, 1998.

Hispanic Education at the Crossroads. Videodisc. Produced by Blue Pearl Entertainment, Written by Rose Marie Arce. Princeton, NJ: Films for the Humanities & Sciences, 2004.

Kloosterman, Valentina I, ed. *Latino Students in American Schools: Historical and Contemporary Views.* Westport, CT: Praeger, 2003.

Krashen, Stephen. *Principles and Practice in Second Language Acquisition.* Oxford: Pergamon Press, 1982.

Leadership Education for Asian Pacifics (LEAP) and Asian Pacific American Public Policy Institute. *The State of Asian Pacific America: Transforming Race Relations.* Los Angeles: LEAP, 2000.

Lee, Stacey J. *Unraveling the "Model Minority" Stereotype: Listening to Asian American Youth.* New York: Teachers College Press, 1996.

Leong, Frederick T.L., L.C. Lee, and Nolan Zane, eds. *Handbook of Asian American Psychology.* Thousand Oaks, CA: Sage, 2007.

McKenna, Teresa, and Flor Ida Ortiz. *The Broken Web: The Educational Experience of Hispanic American Women.* Claremont, CA, Tomas Rivera Center. Berkeley, CA: Floricanto Press, 1988.

Mendez vs. Westminster: For All the Children/ Para Todos Los Ninos. Videocassette. Writer/producer Sandra Robbie. Huntington Beach, CA: KOCE-TV Foundation, 2002.

Nakanishi, Don T. and Tina Y. Nishida, eds. *The Asian American Educational Experience: A Source Book for Teachers and Students.* New York: Routledge, 1995.

National Asian American Telecommunications Association. www.naatanet.org.

Nieto, Sonia. *Affirming Diversity: The Sociopolitical Context of Multicultural Education.* New York: Longman, 2000.

Olsen, Laurie. *Made in America: Immigrant Students in Our Public Schools.* New York: The New Press, 2008.

Pang, Valerie O. and Li-Rong Lilly Cheng, eds. *Struggling to Be Heard: The Unmet Needs of Asian Pacific American Children.* Albany: State University of New York Press, 1998.

Park, Clara C. and Marilyn Mei-Ying Chi, eds. *Asian-American Education: Prospects and Challenge.* Westport, CT: Bergin & Garvey, 1999.

Reyes, Maria de la Luz and John J. Halcon, eds. *The Best for Our Children: Critical Perspectives on Literacy for Latino Students.* New York: Teachers College Press, 2001.

Root, Maria P. P., ed. *The Multiracial Experience: Racial Borders as the New Frontier.* Thousand Oaks, CA: Sage, 1996.

Sandhu, Daya Singh, ed. *Asian and Pacific Islander Americans: Issues and Concerns in Counseling and Psychotherapy.* Huntington, NY: Nova Science Publishers, 1999.

Takaki, Ronald T. *Strangers from a Different Shore: A History of Asian Americans,* rev. ed. New York: Little, Brown, 1998.

Tejeda, Carlos, Corinne Martinez, and Zeus Leonardo, eds. *Charting New Terrains of Chicana(o)/Latina(o) Education*. Cresskill, NJ: Hampton Press, 2000.

Tong, Benson, ed. *Asian American Children: A Historical Guide*. Westport, CT: Greenwood Press, 2004.

Uba, Laura. *Asian Americans: Personality Patterns, Identity, and Mental Health*. New York: Guilford, 1994.

Valdés, Guadalupe. *Learning and Not Learning English: Latino Students in American Schools*. New York: Teachers College Press, 2001.

Valdés, Guadalupe. *Con Respeto: Bridging the Distances between Culturally Diverse Families and Schools*. New York: Teachers College Press, 1996.

Valdés, Guadalupe. *Expanding Definitions of Giftedness: The Case of Young Interpreters from Immigrant Communities*. Mahwah, NJ: Lawrence Erlbaum, 2003.

Vo, Linda T., and Rick Bonus, eds. *Asian American Communities: Intersections and Divergences*. Philadelphia: Temple University Press, 2002.

Wink, Joan. *Critical Pedagogy Note from the Real World*. New York: Addison Wesley Longman, 1997.

Wortham, Stanton, Enrique G. Murillo, Jr., and Edmund T. Hamann, eds. *Education in the New Latino Diaspora: Policy and Politics of Identity*. Westport, CT: Ablex Publishing, 2002.

Ybarra, Raul E. and Nancy Lopez, eds. *Creating Alternative Discourses in the Education of Latinos and Latinas: A Reader*. New York: P. Lang, 2004.

Zentella, Ana Celia. *Building on Strength: Language and Literacy in Latino Families and Communities*. New York: Teachers College Press, 2005.

Zentella, Ana Celia. *Latin @ Languages and Identities*.

Zhou, Min and James V. Gatewood, eds. *Contemporary Asian America: A Multidisciplinary Reader*. New York: New York University Press, 2000.